Wicked Arts Education

Melissa Bremmer, Emiel Heijnen,
Folkert Haanstra

Wicked Arts Education

Designing Creative Programmes

Valiz, Amsterdam

Table of Contents

Introduction

In 2020 we published *Wicked Arts Assignments*: a book with close
to a hundred creative, bold and provocative assignments that were
collected from contemporary arts educators. Although the book
inspired many students, arts teachers and artists, one question
kept coming up: how do you design curricula based on the 'Wicked'
approach? That fundamental question sparked the idea for this book.

Where the book *Wicked Arts Assignments* presented a loose
collection of arts educational recipes, *Wicked Arts Education* is
a full-blown contemporary arts educational cookbook. And yes,
culinary metaphors do seem to be accurate with regard to arts
educational curriculum design[1]: *Wicked Arts Education* helps you
to create exciting arts educational eating experiences, consisting of
varied dishes in a coherent menu. Rather than settling for cookie
cutter art or artistic fast food, this workbook stimulates you to cook
curricula that are experienced as fresh, tailor-made and satisfying.
And finally, *Wicked Arts Education* supports you to cater to
your guests' preferences, acknowledging dietary preferences,
restrictions, or allergies.

This workbook will help you to build arts curricula from scratch,
based on our clear and appealing design model for a Wicked Arts
Curriculum. This model is rooted in academic research and further
developed during the course 'arts educational design' that we have
been teaching at the Amsterdam University of the Arts since 2006.
We also had the chance to test this model and its related strategies
in our curriculum design workshops around the world. Time and

time again we found that *Wicked Arts Education* challenges
arts educators to explore curriculum ideas collectively, creatively
and productively.

But why design Wicked Arts Curricula? Loosely based on
the ideas of Rittel and Webber,[2] we believe that arts education
should revolve around wicked problems and challenges: ambitious,
confusing, messy, complex, and appealing. Arts educational scholar
Olivia Gude already concluded that 'a menu of media, or lists of
domains, modes, and rationales are neither sufficient nor necessary
to inspire a quality art curriculum.'[3] In this workbook, arts teachers
and artists are addressed as the primary agents in the development of high-quality arts curricula. Rather than approaching
educational design solely as a technical exercise, we promote it as
an artistic practice in which creative and systematic approaches
playfully alternate.

In a time of individualization and polarization, we believe in
the power of learning collectively about, in, and through the arts.[4]
Although *Wicked Arts Education* can be used to create personalized
learning trajectories, it advocates building learning communities in
which students and teachers share interests, expertise, and opinions.
Arts classes and other creative learning communities are encountered
as educational microcosms that allow students to experiment, fail
and succeed safely and collectively.

Wicked Arts Education can be used in a variety of educational
contexts: from primary to higher education, and for arts curricula
inside and beyond schools. The use of the term 'arts' underlines
that this workbook is suitable for crafting curricula for the visual
arts, music, dance, theatre, film or design, but also for designing
interdisciplinary arts projects and courses. So, whether you are
a (preservice) arts teacher, an artist, or a curriculum designer, or
if you want to design a single lesson or a complete arts curriculum,
this book is for you!

The *Wicked Arts Education* Manifesto

Wicked Arts Education:

… offers opportunities to learn about ourselves, the arts, and the world. We believe that the arts form historically renowned, specific symbol systems to explore and imagine the world, and their reception and production evoke pleasurable or otherwise remarkable experiences. The arts broaden our horizon because they allow us to encounter stories, people, sounds, images, movements, events, and situations that would otherwise not be part of our daily lives. Moreover, the arts can reveal realities or beliefs and help us to envision and enact 'ways of being together otherwise'.[5, 6]

… appeals to both body and mind. The arts are encountered, made, and understood through complex processes that appeal to our bodies (seeing, feeling, hearing) as well as our minds (interpreting, meaning making, discussing). What we see and experience as 'artistic' is intersubjective and dynamic: it is different all over the world and changes over time. How and what we value as art is part of a social process, an ongoing discourse. This play with form, definitions and meaning is inherent to the arts.

… inspires arts educational design. We believe that artworks can trigger the educational designers' creativity. Works of art are never neutral, they can confront, ask challenging questions, tell stories, show new truths, or take you into other realities. As such, works of art can spark ideas for themes, assignments, materials and techniques for your curriculum.

Designing Wicked Arts Curricula is:

… an artistic practice. Arts curricula often leave much freedom for interpretation. This freedom can be exciting as it allows you to approach educational design as an artistic practice: you can use your imagination and experience to creatively transform your educational ideas into a curriculum.[7] Thus, curricula can emerge with strong personal signatures, in which artistic ideas, pedagogical views and arts practices are integrated in a unique way.

… a collaborative practice. Instead of viewing designing and teaching arts as a solitary activity, we advocate it as an off- or online collaborative practice where a dynamic exchange forms the heart of curriculum development. In a collaborative design practice, teachers can critically discuss their lesson ideas, inspire each other, kill their darlings, and build robust curricula.

… both intuitive and systematic. In some views, curriculum development is seen as a linear process, others see it as a purely holistic endeavour. Yet, we take an in-between stance towards curriculum design. We believe that designing arts education calls for a creative approach that starts intuitively and holistically, but gradually becomes more systematic and analytical.

The Five Design Principles of a Wicked Arts Curriculum:

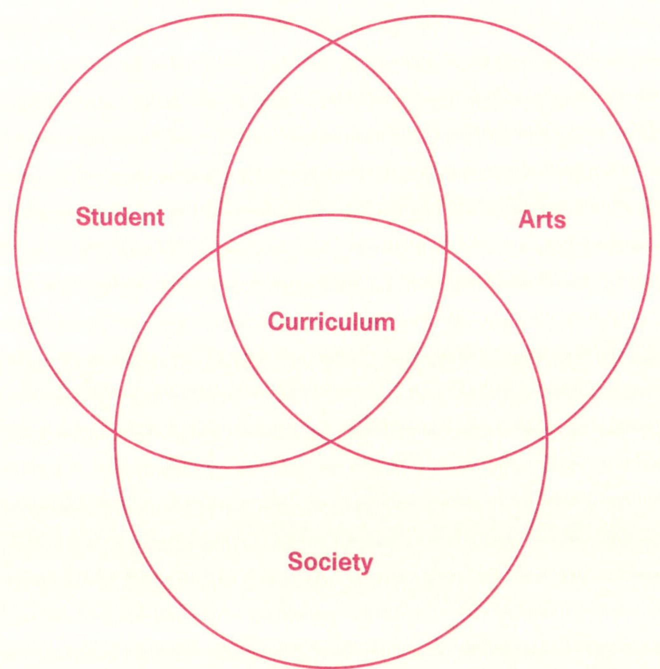

Content
1. Create connections between the domain of the student, the arts and society through themes and sources of inspiration
2. Provide a variety of meaningful materials and techniques

Pedagogy
3. Design *Wicked Arts Assignments* based on enabling constraints
4. Address classes as learning communities, promoting various working strategies and expertises

Contexts for learning
5. Offer opportunities for learning and assessment in lifelike contexts

Reading Guide

The first chapter of this book gives a brief history of the curriculum. In chapter 2 we present the heart of our book: the design model for Wicked Arts Curricula. In that chapter we also provide you with the theoretical backgrounds of *Wicked Arts Education*. In chapter 3 you learn how to make that first, quick intuitive sketch of your curriculum. Then you can push on to chapters 4 to 8 for a systematic overview of different components of curriculum design: learning goals, structure, learning activities, assessment, and evaluation.

NOTES

1   D. Petrovich and R. White, *Draw It with Your Eyes Closed: The Art of the Art Assignment* (Paper Monument, 2012).

2   H. W. J. Rittel and M. M. Webber, 'Dilemmas in a General Theory of Planning', *Policy Sciences*, 4(2) (1973), pp. 155–169.

3   O. Gude, 'Principles of Possibility: Considerations for a 21st-Century Art & Culture Curriculum', *Art Education*, 60(1) (2007), pp. 6–17.

4   S. Neiman, *Left is Not Woke* (John Wiley & Sons, 2023).

5   C. Wild, *Artist-Teacher Practice and the Expectation of an Aesthetic Life: Creative Being in the Neoliberal Classroom* (Routledge, 2022).

6   J. Van Heeswijk, M. Hlavajova and R. Rakes, *Toward the Not-Yet: Art as Public Practice* (BAK, 2021).

7   E. W. Eisner, *The Educational Imagination: On the Design and Evaluation of School Programs* (Macmillan, 1979).

A Brief History of the Curri-culum

In the film installation *Manifesto* (2015) of the German multimedia artist Julian Rosefeldt, famous arts manifestos are delivered by Cate Blanchett in thirteen different roles and settings, creating surrealistic scenes. For example, we see Blanchett as a fifth-grade teacher, giving a lecture to her students. Walking around the class, she checks if the children write down the Danish filmmakers Dogme 95 text correctly in their notebooks: 'The camera must be hand-held…'

A manifesto is a written statement publicly declaring the position of its issuer. It advances a set of ideas, but it can also lay out a plan of action. In the arts, many manifestos initially provoked confusion, laughter, or anger, but proved to be game-changers. Such as: 'We don't wanna assimilate to someone else's (boy) standards' in punk band Bikini Kill's *Riot grrrl manifesto* (1991), 'No virtuosity' in choreographer Yvonne Rainer's *No Manifesto* (1965), or 'We abolish the stage and the auditorium' in Antonin Artaud's *Theatre of Cruelty* (1964). Just like arts movements, arts curricula are never ideology-free. They build on underlying concepts and ideas that are sometimes presented with the same panache as our *Wicked Arts Education* Manifesto. In this chapter we discuss the different levels of curricula, their underlying visions, and what colour, shape and content they can take on.

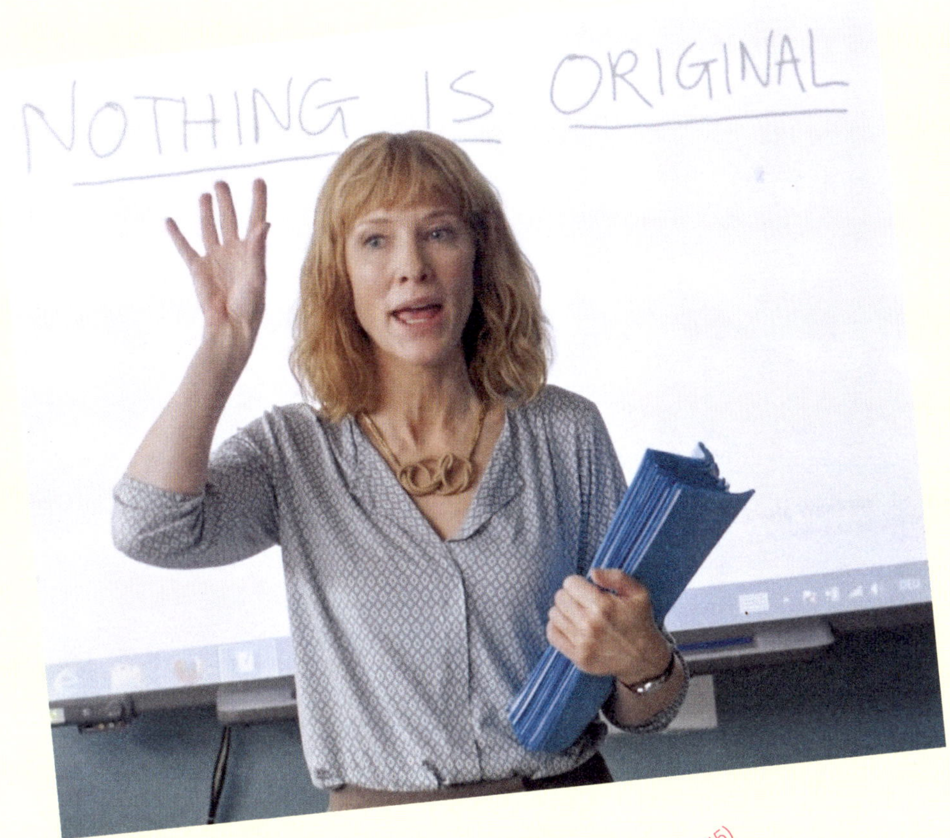

Julian Rosefeldt, Manifesto (2015)

Contents of this chapter

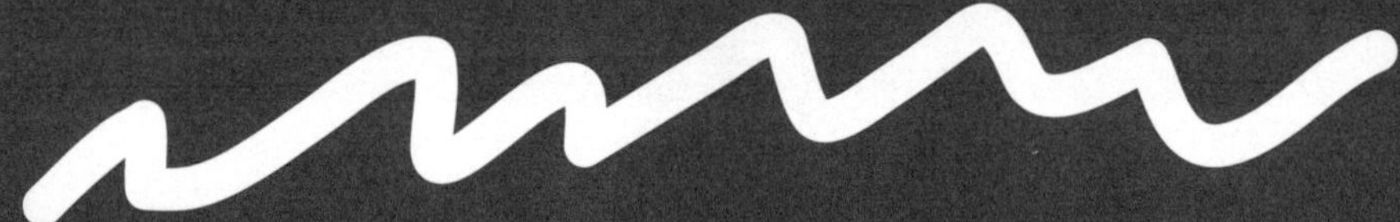

1.1   What Is a Curriculum?

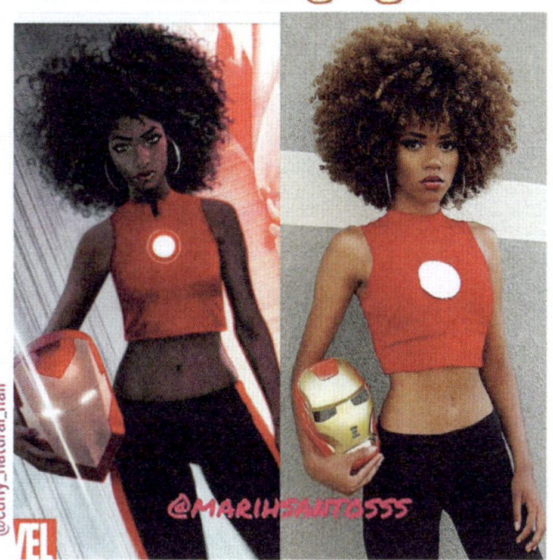

Informal learning: Online feedback on a Cosplay character based on Marvel's *Ironheart*

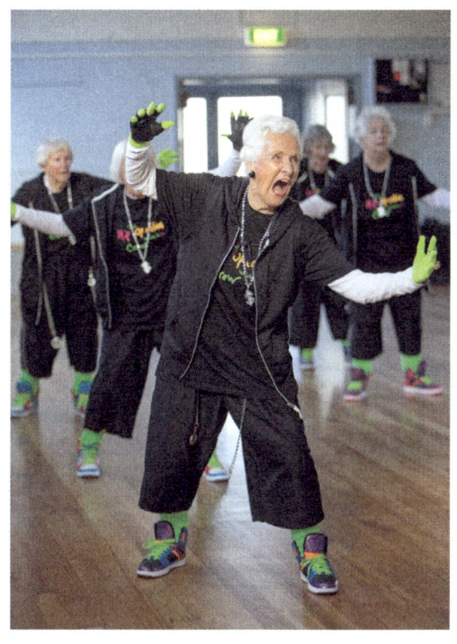

Non-formal learning: The Hip-Hop-eration Crew, Waiheke, New Zealand
Photo: Peter Meecham

When you think up an arts assignment, activity, or course, you are, willingly or not, designing a chunk of curriculum. The word curriculum has historically yielded many meanings and associations. In Arabic, it is associated with listing and ordering.[1] In Latin, however, the verb *currere* means to run, and curriculum refers both to a 'course' and a 'vehicle'. Today, curriculum is mostly associated with schools and other educational institutes (formal learning). But the many online DIY video manuals that people use at home to learn how to play guitar or to make a stunning Cosplay outfit are just as well pieces of curriculum (informal learning). Curricula are also found in the hybrid space between informal and formal learning. So-called non-formal learning situations are situated outside schools, usually guided by experts, and materialized in the form of courses, apprenticeships or educational programmes of cultural institutes.[2]

Wicked Arts Education is, in the first place, aimed at formal learning contexts, from primary to higher education. It can also be applied in the context of non-formal learning situations, like music/dance/theatre schools or museum education. We therefore define curriculum as a plan for learning, based on the Estonian-American curriculum theorist Taba.[3] A plan for learning resonates with the German *Lehrplan*, the Swedish *läroplan* and the Dutch term *leerplan*.[4]

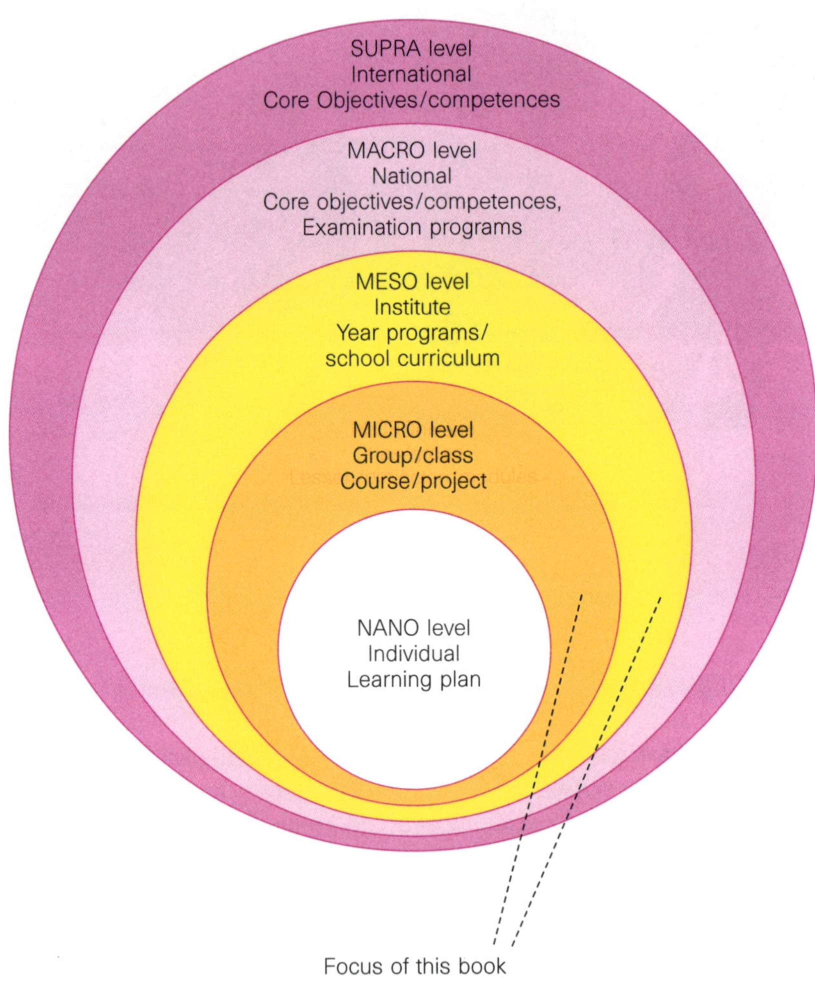

Curriculum levels and products, and the focus of *Wicked Arts Education*

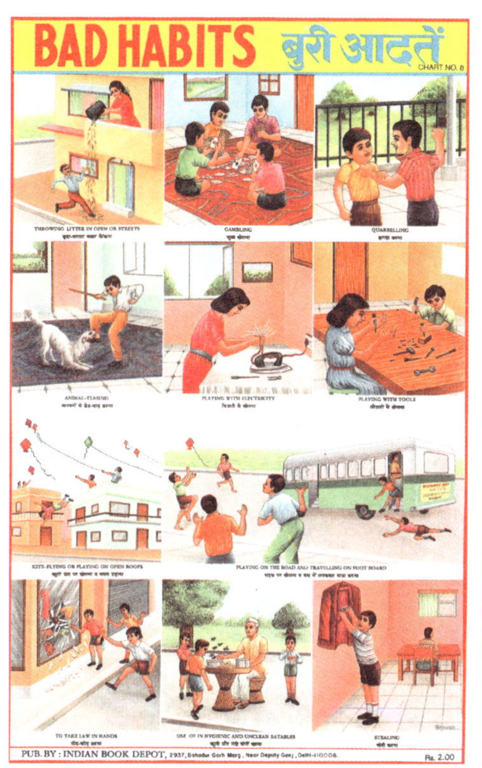

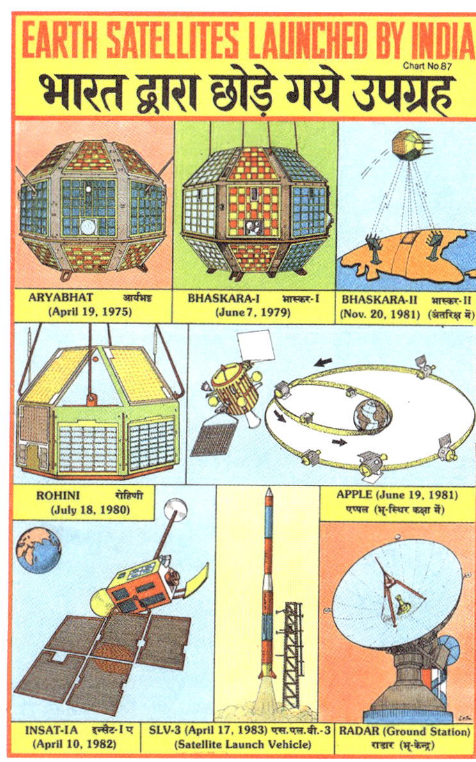

After India's independence in 1947, schools would put up charts in their classroom that shed light on their intended curriculum

A plan for learning in the arts can be applied to different curricular levels. From a personalized plan for learning to play Spanish guitar at the nano level, to the Common European Framework of Reference for Visual Literacy at the supra level.[5] This book focuses on curriculum design at both the micro and meso level. At the micro level, it offers guidance for the design of an arts educational course or project for a particular student group or class. It can also be used for the design of arts curricula at the meso level, consisting of multiple courses/projects over a longer period (e.g. a semester, a year).

1.2 Curriculum Manifestations

Curricula can not only be found in different contexts or at different levels, the same curriculum manifests itself also in various forms — on different moments and for different stakeholders. A teacher may find the theatre course challenging on paper, but students may find its implementation boring and too simple. Van den Akker describes a threefold common typology for these different curriculum manifestations: the *intended*, the *implemented*, and the *attained* curriculum.[6]

The intended curriculum specifies the intention of the learning plan before it is implemented: what *should* the student do and learn? It manifests itself in the form of a rationale or basic learning philosophy: the *ideal curriculum*, and in the form of written curriculum documents or materials: the *formal curriculum*.

The way a learning plan is interpreted and performed is called the implemented curriculum: what are the teachers and students *doing*? This phase deals with how the intended curriculum is interpreted and performed by its users, especially teachers. This manifestation presents itself in the form of the *curriculum-in-action*, the observable process of teaching and learning, and all the activities that happen around it.

The attained curriculum concerns the (learning) experiences that an implemented learning plan generates: what does the programme *bring about*? From this perspective, the knowledge, understanding, skills and attitudes that students actually develop through teaching and learning (both intended and unintended) are identified. The attained curriculum can be determined in different ways: by tests or demonstrations in practice (see chapter 7).

Theoretically, the intended, implemented, and attained curricula are identical. The teacher or educational designer's holy grail is that the intention of a plan for learning is implemented accordingly and results in the desired learning results. Of course, this is seldom the case—and it is one of the aspects that makes education and its design so vibrant and interesting…. and sometimes frustrating. Apart from these common forms in which curricula present themselves, we want to include a curricular manifestation that is more controversial because it resides in the shadows of official curricula. The *Hidden Curriculum* was first described by Jackson in 1968,[7] who recognized that educational settings also produce informal, implicit, and sometimes undesired forms of knowledge,

behaviours and values.[8] Hidden Curricula manifest themselves
in various ways, such as through teaching and learning styles,
emphasis on learning contents, dominant narratives, and the
architecture of the learning environment.

An example of a Hidden Curriculum in dance education is
described by Stinson.[9] She found that in some dance courses
students are expected to 'obediently follow directions, to stay "on
task", to avoid chatting with other students or attending to any
personal needs except those that are most pressing'. While this is
a renowned teaching method of professional choreographers, it does
not provide space for the individuality and creativity of (mainly
female) amateur students. The fact that boys are nearly absent
in the classes reinforce the idea that obedience is a feature that
girls in particular need to learn.

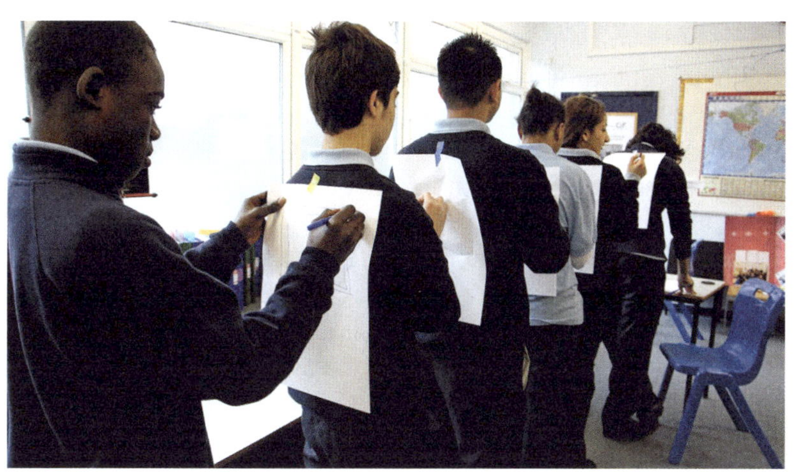

Annette Krauss, *Hidden Curriculum* (2007 >)

An intriguing example of a Hidden Curriculum that students
themselves create and maintain, is studied by artist Annette
Krauss. Her project *Hidden Curriculum* (2007 >) documents the
practices and coping strategies that teen students use and share in
their everyday school life. For example, students have documented
in videos how stairs, handrails, lockers, and school furniture can
be used in non-standard ways. Krauss also collects and documents
the various tricks and excuses that high school students in different
countries mutually share to cheat at tests or to skip school.[10]

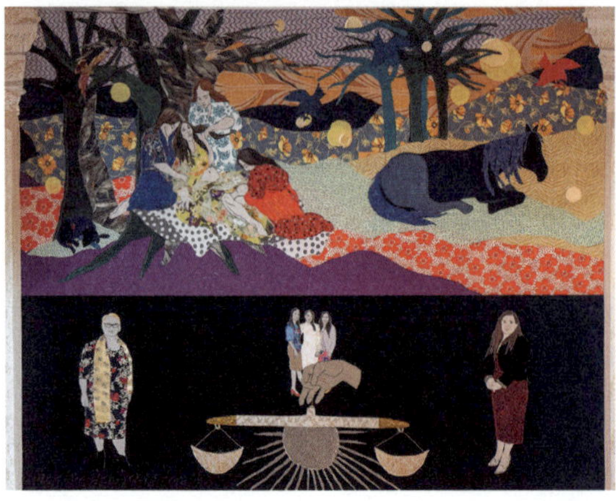

Małgorzata Mirga-Tas, *Re-enchanting the World* (fragment) (2022). Mirga-Tas was the first Romani artist to have her work represented in a national pavilion (Poland) at the Biennale di Venezia (2022). The tapestry installation *Re-enchanting the World* expands European iconography and art history with representations of Roma culture

As no course or curriculum has an infinite amount of time and space, every curriculum is always based on the question of what *is* included and what is *not*. The Null Curriculum[11] is everything that is absent or not taught in a programme, signifying all that is deemed as unessential, unimportant, or invisible. Apt examples of typical Null Curricula in the arts are traditional art history narratives that present a 'canon' in which non-western art, BIPoC (Black, Indigenous and people of colour) and female artists are nearly absent (a striking example above).

Before you engage in the process of constructing a new piece of curriculum, a valuable exercise may be to ask yourself and your colleagues what kind of hidden or Null Curricula already exist in your school/institute. Exploring the knowledge, behaviours and values that are *implicit* or *missing*, can help you to shed light on your intended curriculum.

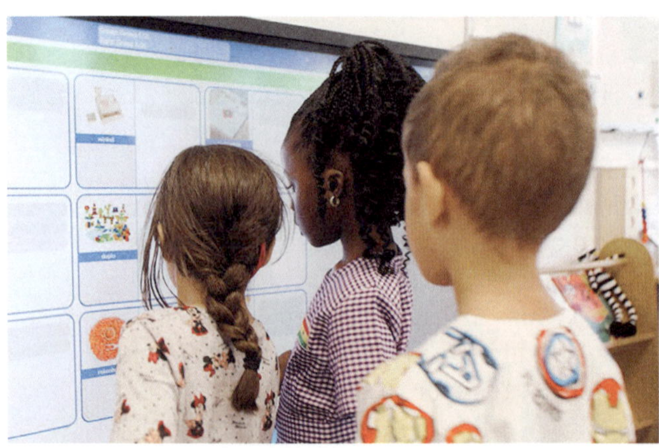

Planning board as used in Dalton schools, where students typically make their own weekly planning

1.3 Curriculum Visions

Either implicit or explicit, each curriculum has an underlying rationale of *what* has to be learned and *how* learning goals can be achieved.[12] There are many educational concepts or learning philosophies that are used to underpin an ideal curriculum, such as Montessori or Dalton, personalized learning, or problem-based learning. These different curriculum rationales can roughly be divided into three global visions on learning: *disciplined-centred*, *learner-centred* and *society-centred*.[13]

The Discipline-Centred Curriculum

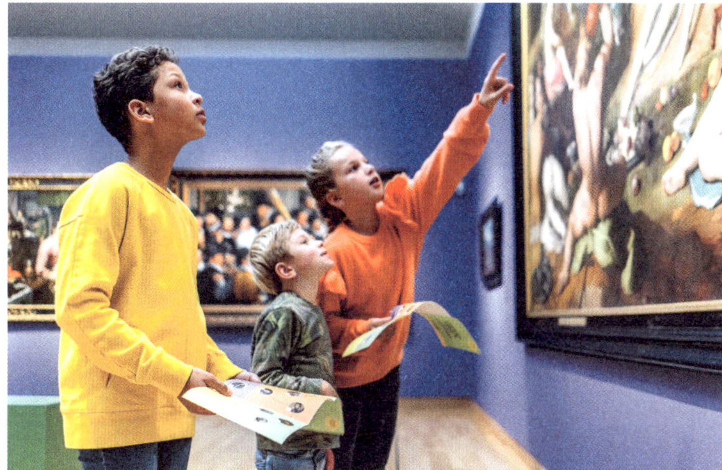

Art history and art criticism are important aspects of DBAE. Photo: Frans Hals Museum (2021)

The main goal of this vision is to increase the learner's knowledge based on academic disciplines such as mathematics, philosophy, or science. Curricula are subject-based and aim to teach students discipline-specific knowledge, skills, and behaviours. Teachers are seen as highly skilled experts in their discipline and formal examinations can play a big role in the assessment of learning.

Example in the arts: *Discipline-Based Art Education* was developed by the Getty Center for Education in the Arts as a critique of secondary art education that overemphasizes aspects like expression and studio production.[14] DBAE promotes a sequential art curriculum based on four disciplines: art production, art history, art criticism and aesthetics.

The Learner-Centred Curriculum

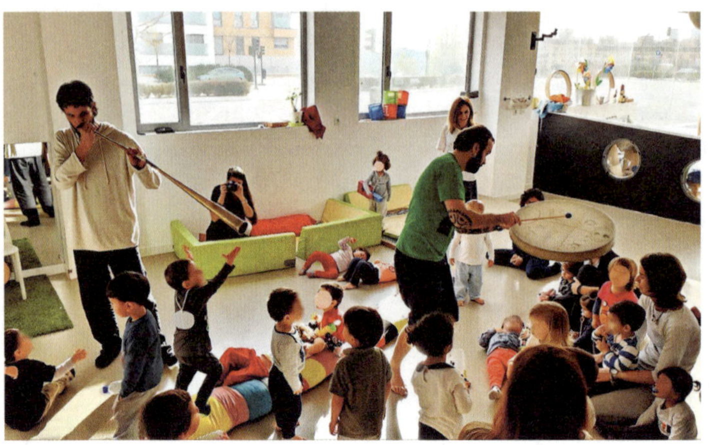

Atelieristas at work in a Reggio Emilia class at the Escuela Infantil Reggio in Madrid, Spain (2016)

In this vision, the interests and needs of the learner are the cornerstone. Learning is geared towards the student's personal growth and development. The teacher is mainly considered a coach or facilitator who is able to flexibly tailor the curriculum to the student's learning needs. As (self)discovery plays an important role, assessment often has a formative character.

Example in the arts: in Reggio Emilia pedagogy the expressive arts and the guidance by specialist arts teachers (*atelieristas*) play a central role in learning.[15] Reggio preschool educators believe that every child has a fundamental right to realize and expand their potential. Much attention is given to detailed observation and documentation of the students' learning process, rather than on learning outcomes.

The Society-Centred Curriculum

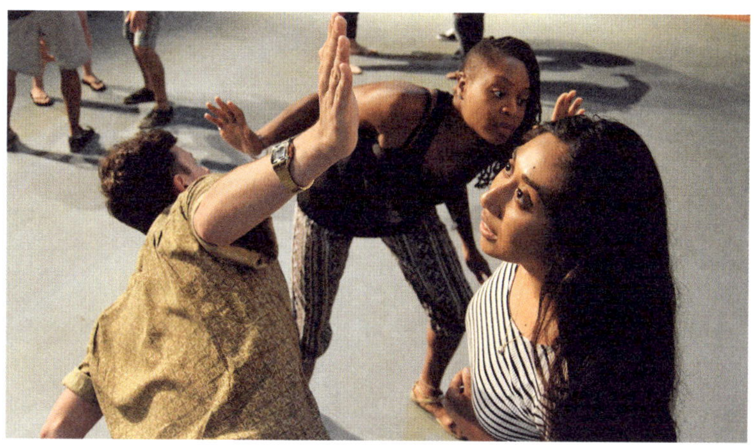

Theatre of the Oppressed scene about racism in Brazil (2015)
Courtesy of Robert Gordon

Social relevancy is a central concern in these curricula, which can be interpreted in two directions: the *social adaptation* and the *social reconstruction* vision. From the viewpoint of social adaptation, curricula should help students acquire the skills needed to fit in society. For instance, creativity is an important skill for complex and increasingly digitized societies and arts education is mentioned as a subject area that can foster this skill.[16]

The *social reconstruction* vision is aimed at raising critical citizens. Societal challenges and real-world problems should be discovered and resolved throughout the curriculum, educating students to think and act as (critical) citizens. Students are approached as community members who collectively study inter-disciplinary content matter. Teachers have to be skilled in facilitating teamwork and collaborative learning. Assessment is often aimed at the application of knowledge and skills in lifelike contexts.

Example in the arts: the *Theatre of the Oppressed* is a form of community-based education that uses theatre as a tool for social and political transformation.[17] By overthrowing the opposition between actors and spectators, 'spect-actors' get the opportunity to both act and observe, fostering processes of dialogue and critical thinking.

1.4   Integrating Curriculum Visions

Tyler integrates a discipline-, learner-, and society-centred curriculum vision in the same model.[18] This model extends Dewey's 1897 assertion that academic knowledge lacks significance if it does not connect with the learner's experiences and the world beyond school.[19, 20] The idea that a school curriculum should respond to all three dimensions is the foundation of Tyler's curriculum rationale. Hence, a balanced curriculum should be informed by three types of sources: the knowledge and skills derived from *professional disciplines*, the values, aims and attitudes of a democratic *society* and the *learner's* competencies, interests, and needs.

Tyler's threefold integration of curriculum visions resonates with Biesta's contemporary interpretation of the key functions of education: *qualification, socialization*, and *subjectification*.[21] Qualification provides children and young people with the knowledge and skills they will need as future citizens and employees. Socialization prepares students for their lives as members of a community and how to become part of existing traditions and social, cultural, and political orders. Subjectification, finally, is aimed at the development of the student as individuals, discovering aspects such as passions and beliefs, autonomy and responsibilities. Like Tyler, Biesta presents the design and implementation of a curriculum as a balancing act in which discipline-, society- and learner-centred approaches are seen as intertwined dimensions that are in continuous dialogue with each other.

Next Up: The Design Model for Wicked Arts Curricula

This has been a quick dive into the history of the curriculum. In our next chapter, we will present the design model for Wicked Arts Curricula, the basis for your curriculum design. It draws explicitly on Dewey's principles of meaningful learning and it incorporates Tyler's three dimensions: discipline, student, and society. Additionally, it is heavily influenced by the educational concepts of Authentic Arts Education and Universal Design for Learning — all explained in the following chapter.

NOTES

1 C. G. Yaşar and B. Aslan, 'Curriculum Theory: A Review Study', *International Journal of Curriculum and Instructional Studies*, 11(2) (2021), pp. 237–260.

2 J. A. Vadeboncoeur, 'Engaging Young People: Learning in Informal Contexts', *Review of Research in Education*, 30(1) (2006), pp. 239–278.

3 H. Taba, *Curriculum Development: Theory and Practice* (Harcourt Publishers Group, 1962).

4 A. Thijs and J. van den Akker (eds.), *Curriculum in Development* (Netherlands Institute for Curriculum Development, 2009).

5 E. Wagner and D. Schönau, *Common European Framework of Reference for Visual Literacy — Prototype* (Waxmann, 2016).

6 J. van den Akker, 'Curriculum Perspectives: An Introduction', in J. J. H. Van den Akker, W. A. J. M. Kuiper and U. Hameyer (eds.), *Curriculum Landscapes and Trends* (Kluwer Academic Publishers, 2003), pp. 1–10.

7 P. W. Jackson, *Life in Classrooms* (Teachers College Press, 1990).

8 M. A. Alsubaie, 'Hidden Curriculum as One of Current Issue of Curriculum', *Journal of Education and Practice*, 6(33) (2015), pp. 125–128.

9 S. W. Stinson, 'The Hidden Curriculum of Gender in Dance Education', *Journal of Dance Education*, 5(2), (2005), pp. 51–57.

10 A. Krauss, *Hidden Curriculum* (project website, 2014), www.hidden-curriculum.info.

11 E. W. Eisner, *The Educational Imagination* (Macmillan, 1979).

12 D. Georgescu, 'Curriculum Philosophies for the 21st Century: What is Old and What is New?', in Crisan, A. (ed.) *Current and Future Challenges in Curriculum Development: Policies, Practices and Networking for Change* (Editura Educatia 2000+ Humanitas Educational, 2006), pp. 79–96.

13 A. K. Ellis, *Exemplars of Curriculum Theory* (Routledge, 2004).

14 S. M. Dobbs, *The DBAE Handbook: An Overview of Discipline-Based Art Education* (Oxford University Press, 1992).

15 C. Edwards, L. Gandini and G. Forman (eds.), 'The Hundred Languages of Children', *Elsevier Science, 2nd edition* (Elsevier Science, 1998).

16   S. Vincent-Lancrin, C. Gonzales, M. Bouckaert, F. De Luca, M. Fernandez, G. Jacotin, J. Urgels and Q. Vidal, 'Fostering Students' Creativity and Critical Thinking: What it Means in School', *Educational Research and Innovation* (OECD Publishing, 2019).

17   A. Boal, *Theatre of the Oppressed* (Theatre Communications Group, 1993).

18   R. W. Tyler, *Basic Principles of Curriculum and Instruction* (University of Chicago Press, 1949).

19   J. Dewey, *The School and Society* (University of Chicago Press, 1907).

20   Z. Deng and A. Luke, 'Subject Matter: Defining and Theorizing School Subjects', in F. M. Connelly, M. F. He and J. Phillion (eds.), *The SAGE Handbook of Curriculum and Instruction* (Sage Publications, 2008), pp. 66–87.

21   G. Biesta, *Good Education in an Age of Measurement: Ethics, Politics, Democracy* (Paradigm Publishers, 2010).

Design Model for Wicked Arts Curricula

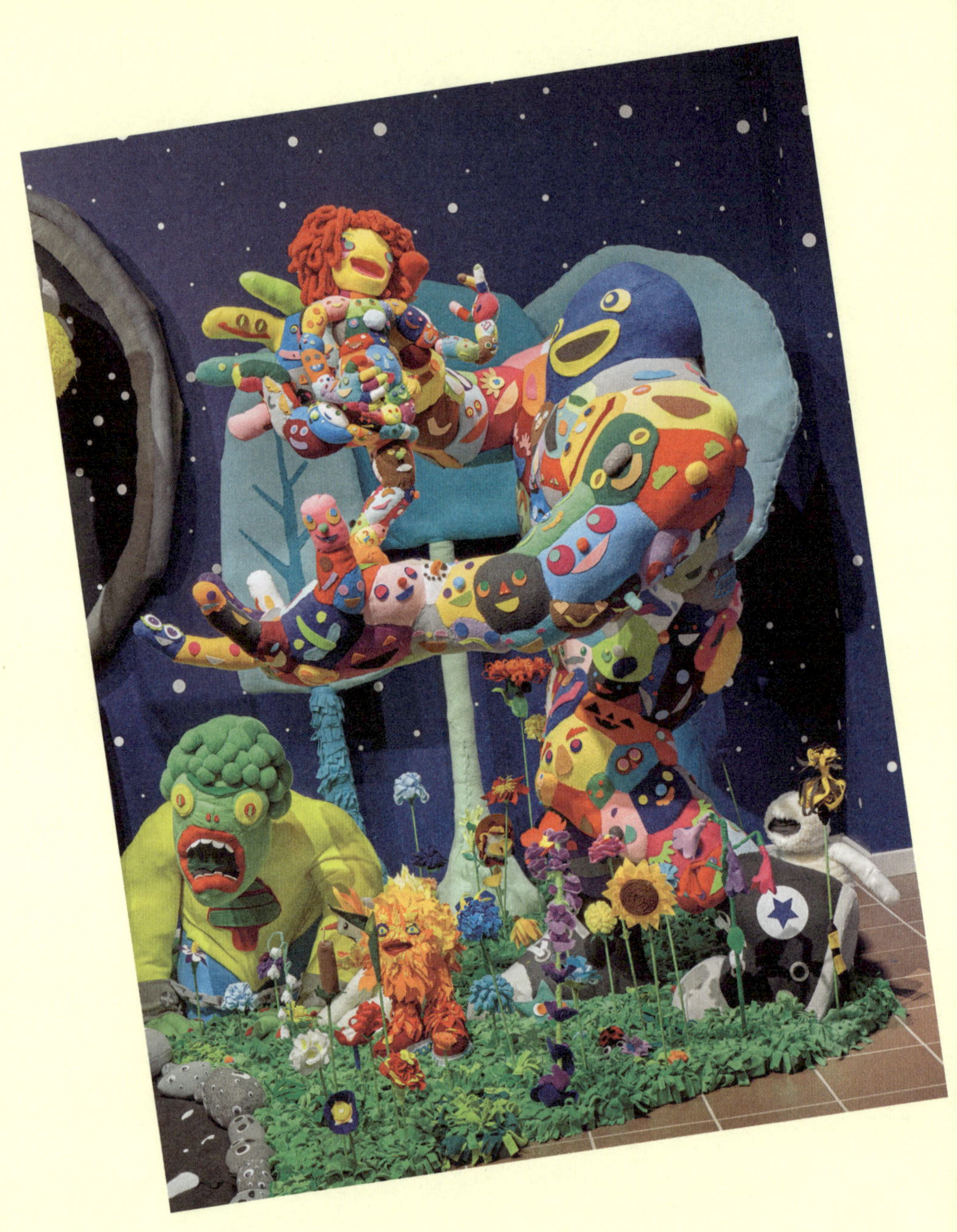

JooYoung Choi, *Like a Bolt out of the Blue, Faith Steps in and Sees You Through* (2019), detail featuring Poundcake Man, Emma Poundcake Girl and Lady Madness

In a colourful tsunami of visual storytelling, multidisciplinary Korean-American artist JooYoung Choi drags you into her fictional land, the Cosmic Womb. Just like in *Wicked Arts Education*, popular culture, societal themes, and the arts meet each other in JooYoung's work. Her eccentric sci-fi characters were inspired by the tv shows and trading cards of the artist's childhood. The themes of identity, loss, and healing that JooYoung explores form the societal component of the work. The Cosmic Womb is an inclusive community of over 250 characters, each with distinct traits and a unique backstory. For instance, there is the green-skinned villain Lady Madness; the Pound Cake Man, a giant collective entity formed by Globbernauts; and Nina Blue, a pansexual professional imaginary friend. The arts are manifest through the artist's skill and idiom, displayed by means of painting, video, sculpture, animation, music and installations. The use of mixed media offers the audience a variety of entry points into the Cosmic Womb, just as we propose that *Wicked Arts Education* should cater to a variety of learners. Transforming all these influences, stories, and materials to a cohesive whole is a craft that JooYoung Choi has clearly mastered. Feel inspired by JooYoung and use the design model for Wicked Arts Curricula to sculpt a vibrant arts curriculum!

Contents of this chapter

2.1 The Design Model

The design model for Wicked Arts Curricula guides you in designing arts curricula, spanning brief courses to year-long arts programmes. Because the model is flexible, it can be applied in numerous learning contexts within and beyond schools. You will see that the model is formed by three intersecting domains: the student (the learner's competencies, interests, and needs), the arts (knowledge and skills derived from professional disciplines), and society (societal themes). We believe that the central area in the model (see next page) forms the ideal site for Wicked Arts Curricula. Here the three domains overlap, representing a curriculum that strives for meaningful connections with the culture of the student, the arts and society. This connection also stresses that there is no strict hierarchy between traditional divisions such as popular and high arts, amateur and professional arts, or applied and autonomous arts.

In the first part of this chapter we will explain each of these domains, showing how these inform the content, context and pedagogy of Wicked Arts Curricula. In the second part we will take a closer look at the theoretical foundations of *Wicked Arts Education*.

Student

The domain of the student is formed by their specific culture, knowledge, skills, and interests. The content of this domain is to a great extent influenced by art expressions of popular culture, mass media, vernacular art and subcultures that students encounter in their daily lives. When students are actively performing and creating for instance music, or dances, they develop informal working strategies and skills in relation to the use of specific techniques and materials. The contexts in which students learn these working strategies and skills are informal too: at home, on the street and increasingly in the digital realm of the Internet. The knowledge, skills, and taste that students develop are always influenced by the social context in which they participate: their family members, the friends they hang out with online and offline, and the peers that inspire them. Arts educators who implement Wicked Arts Curricula are challenged to draw on this domain in class. This requires a pedagogy that offers students (a degree of) autonomy and choice,

Content
- Expressions of popular culture, mass media, vernacular art and subcultures
- Informal working strategies, materials and techniques

Pedagogy
- Teaching students to employ their (cultural) backgrounds and personal knowledge, skills, feelings, ideas and opinions

Contexts for learning
- Locations: home, public space, web
- Social: family, friends, peers

Content
- Expressions of arts and design
- Professional working strategies, materials and techniques

Pedagogy
- Teaching students to think and work like artists, performers, designers, critics, etc.

Contexts tor learning
- Locations: theatres, concert halls, museums, galleries, cinemas, studios, public space, web
- Social: the arts world

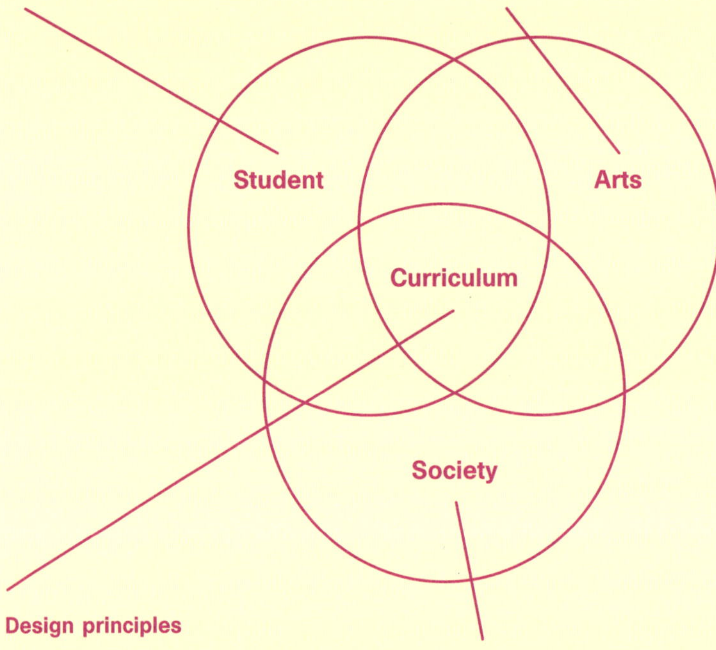

Design principles

Content
1. Create connections between the domain of the student, the arts and society through themes and sources of inspiration
2. Provide a variety of meaningful materials and techniques

Pedagogy
3. Design Wicked Arts Assignments based on enabling constraints
4. Address classes as learning communities, promoting different working strategies and expertise

Contexts for learning
5. Offer opportunities for learning and assessment in lifelike contexts

Content
- Stories, (local) histories, opinions, problems, events, actualities

Pedagogy
- Teaching students to relate to broad societal perspectives

Contexts for learning
- All physical and social contexts beyond the arts

enabling them to employ their (cultural) backgrounds and personal knowledge, skills, feelings, ideas and opinions in assignments, courses, and projects.

Arts

The domain of the arts includes the discipline-specific knowledge, skills, and attitudes that are common among arts professionals. The content of this domain is formed by expressions of arts and design, such as plays, artworks, songs, choreographies, films, and 2D and 3D design objects. It also includes the expressions that describe, document or discuss the arts world in books, magazines and reviews. Also important here are the working strategies, materials, and techniques that professionals in the arts apply. Providing students access to the domain of the arts requires a pedagogy aimed at *disciplined inquiry*.[1,2] This entails that students learn to think and act as professionals in different arts disciplines: as artists, performers, designers, curators, arts theorists and critics. Disciplined inquiry is not necessarily aimed at training students to become arts professionals, but it enables them to experience how art works through multiple entry points: through the process of immersion, identification, and confrontation. Ideally, the context for disciplined inquiry is located in the artworld itself, for instance in a studio, a theatre, museum, or the public space in which an artistic intervention takes place, and in close contact with artists and other representatives of the arts world.

Society

The domain of society represents broad societal themes that are reflected in the culture of the student and the arts. Its content is formed by histories, opinions, problems and (political) actualities that can generate actual themes for Wicked Arts Curricula. Consequently, teachers will employ a pedagogy that relates the arts to a broad variety of societal themes, inviting students to creatively and critically examine their personal perspectives on these themes. This pedagogy underlines that the arts are not isolated, but affiliated with other domains such as philosophy, history, science, economy, and politics. As such, societal themes provide a conceptual and contextual framework for artistic exploration. The context of these themes varies. They can be found on both a local and global level, and in all physical and social contexts beyond the arts.

Curriculum

The space where the three domains overlap represents a curriculum that strives for meaningful connections with the culture of the student, the arts, and society. Therefore, the content of a Wicked Arts Curriculum is usually designed around one or several themes that combine the domain of the *student, arts*, and *society*. To offer students multiple entry points to understand a theme, arts educators can use different inspirational sources derived from these three domains. Teachers will also provide students with a variety of materials and techniques. Materials and techniques become meaningful to students when they are not typically 'school-like', but when they relate to the domains of the student or society and the arts.

An important part of the pedagogy of *Wicked Arts Education* is the use of Wicked Arts Assignments. These types of assignments are holistic, because they are not divided into small sub-tasks for the students like a manual or a recipe. Furthermore, Wicked Arts Assignments are based on *enabling constraints*: a set of constraints that open up possibilities by limiting choices (e.g. certain materials, a specific theme, a time limitation), thus providing students a midway between an open and closed assignment. Such an assignment widens the scope for students' initiative, autonomy and exploration and provides some direction for the creative process, but does not prescribe an end product.

Another important part of a Wicked Arts pedagogy is that the class operates as a learning community. This also means that it is seen as a productive, collaborative environment in which diverse working strategies are promoted, and different forms of expertise of students and the teacher are shared. Therefore, group work, student consultation, presentations and (peer) assessments are regular features of the learning process.

Lastly, to make learning meaningful, students should be given opportunities for learning and assessment in realistic contexts. These contexts for learning are based on the lifelike locations and situations in which arts practitioners usually operate. Lifelike contexts for learning are realized when a (part of) a curriculum takes place beyond school, for instance, as a field trip, or as dance lessons at the local theatre. However, lifelike contexts for learning and assessment can also be achieved inside schools, for instance, when students are given the opportunity to work with professional film equipment, or when arts professionals co-assess their work.

The Five Design Principles for Wicked Arts Curricula

The five design principles that form the centre of the model are the basis for the design of a Wicked Arts Curriculum. They offer you and your colleagues support during the design process, and challenge you to create innovative lessons and courses that are meaningful and accessible to all types of students.

<u>Content</u>
1. Create connections between the domain of the *student*, the *arts* and *society* through themes and sources of inspiration
2. Provide a variety of meaningful materials and techniques

<u>Pedagogy</u>
3. Design Wicked Arts Assignments based on enabling constraints
4. Address classes as learning communities, promoting various working strategies and expertises

<u>Contexts for learning</u>
5. Offer opportunities for learning and assessment in lifelike contexts

2.2 Foundations of *Wicked Arts Education*

As we mentioned in chapter one, all curricula are implicitly or explicitly informed by theories, concepts, and models on what and how we think students (should) learn. *Wicked Arts Education* is no different. It distinguishes itself from traditional, craft-centred arts curricula, also known as school art. Furthermore, it is based on Authentic Arts Education and *Universal Design for Learning (UDL)*. Both Authentic Arts Education and UDL are rooted in social-constructivist theories of learning, and stress that learning is connected both to the student's personal worlds and the professional and societal worlds beyond the school. In this part of the chapter we will delve more deeply into school art and Authentic Arts Education, and UDL.

Authentic Arts Education

School Arts

Authentic Arts Education is a pedagogical approach that criticizes the anachronistic nature of traditional arts education and advocates a lively and meaningful curriculum by blurring the boundaries between the world of school and the 'real' world. Yet, what are the characteristics of traditional arts education? In his classic article 'The School Art Style' the American art educator Efland wrote: 'Art teachers need to face the fact that what is frequently taken to be the content of the art that is made in school is not about art as it exists beyond the school; it may be more a function of the school life-style itself.'[3] School art products must be made in a short time with easily applied materials, which should be easily cleaned and stored. The products should look childlike, and are often decorative, disconnected from contemporary art, formulaic, and apparently free of cognitive strain. Bresler studied school music in primary education and her findings are similar to those of Efland.[4] She writes how topics in music (like in dance, drama and visual art and unlike 'academic' subjects) revolve around the calendar holidays (such as Christmas), seasons (e.g. autumn, spring) and special events (e.g. school assemblies). Students often use easy to play instruments, such as xylophones and boomwhackers to play a repertoire that is adapted to school settings.[5] In short: this 'school arts style' primarily serves to celebrate school functions, to offer students a joyful break from more theoretical school subjects and to lend schools a 'humanistic' appearance.[6]

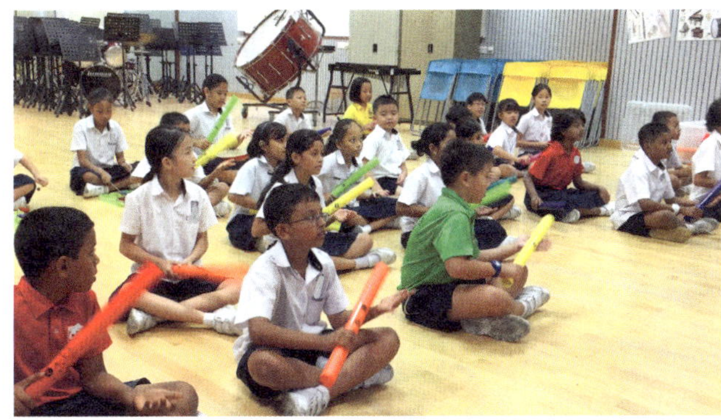

Music class with boom-whackers at the Peiying Primary School, Singapore (2024)

Aspects of school arts are also visible in secondary schools, although in other forms because of the higher status of arts subjects in the curriculum and the presence of specialized arts teachers. Green found that most British music teachers do use popular music in their lessons.[7] It is not their content that she criticizes (although teachers often use pop music from their own younger years) but the way music is taught. In formal music education, teachers mostly choose the music and set out learning trajectories from simple to complex. Learning takes place through notation, instructions, or exercises. By contrast, informal music learning outside school starts with the music the participants choose for themselves and the main method for informal music learning is by listening and copying recordings. Listening, playing, singing, improvising, and composing are integrated and take place in friendship groups with minimum adult guidance. According to Green, these informal learning practices are possible and desirable in a classroom context, because when pop styles are taught via traditional methods, they lose their authenticity as they become a kind of classical music for the students.

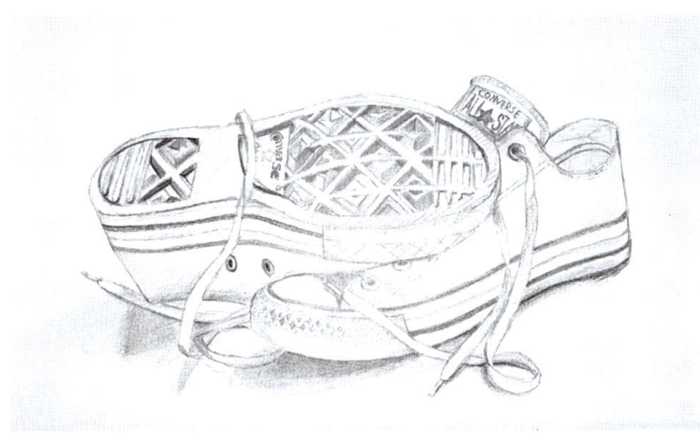

Charlotta (11th grade), *Draw Your Own Sneaker*, Erich Kästner Gemeinschaftsschule, Barsbüttel, Germany (2023)

With respect to visual arts in secondary education Atkinson and Gude have stated that the artistic and pedagogical views of teachers are often deeply rooted in modernist ideas, such as an emphasis on formalistic visual research as a method to amplify the student's capacity for 'self-expression' and 'originality'.[8, 9] In such curricula, traditional media and modernist art examples are dominant, and expression, formal aesthetics and technical skills are emphasized as more important than the construction of meaning and creative research (see the sneaker drawing on page 39). Harland found that this view is recognizable across the different arts subjects in secondary schools.[10] Data from various empirical studies in the UK revealed that the focus in dance, music, visual arts and music lessons was on techniques and skills, rather than on 'exploring and expressing meaning in or through the arts'.[11] Vermeersch and Elias explain that this approach reduces the arts to lower thinking skills such as memorizing and imitating.[12] A contemporary arts curriculum should not only focus on performing or *doing* art: *how do I make it?* It should—in line with contemporary artists—focus more on forms of creative and critical thinking: *'why do I make it?'*

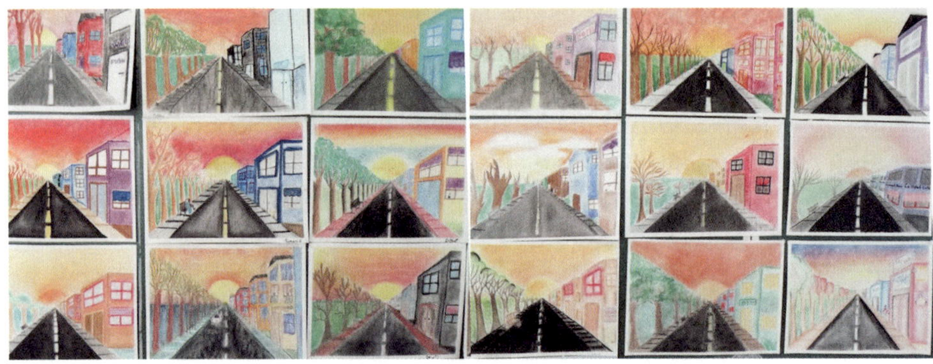

Perspective assignment, Stellenbosch Waldorf School, South Africa (2021)

Publications by experts from different countries illustrate that the school art(s) style is still influential in school curricula all over the globe, from North Europe[13] to Singapore,[14] and from Brazil[15] to New Zealand.[16] A world-wide questionnaire amongst teachers on the content of arts education[17] showed that 'non-canonical arts' e.g., tattooing, commercials, computer games, entertainment, were rated lowest on average. 'Cultural heritage', 'crafts' and 'classical high arts' were endorsed most. Similarly, Wilson wrote how art teachers in the US 'are typically stuck in the past', limiting their curriculum to classical and modern art.[18] Other teachers may supplement the traditional curricula with contemporary artistic sources, but do not change the traditional modernist goals of their curricula. According to Wilson this drains those sources 'from their most potent educational quality—their exploration of the contemporary world, its concerns and ideological pursuits.'[19]

Again and again, critical arts educators such as Steers have underlined the anachronistic character of such curricula, that are both out of sync with contemporary arts practice and do not cater to the students' interests (see the perspective assignment to the left).[20] This gap between school and 'real life' is an old problem. As early as 1907 Dewey wrote: 'From the standpoint of the child, the great waste in the school comes from his inability to utilize the experiences he gets outside the school in any complete and free way within the school itself; while, on the other hand, he is unable to apply in daily life what he is learning at school. That is the isolation of the school—its isolation from life'.[21]

Authentic Learning

As the isolation of school curricula is an old problem, there is a tradition of educational reform movements that try to close the gap between school and the world. These movements are often based on the learning principles of social constructivism, in which two perspectives from learning psychology are united: constructivism and situated learning. According to constructivism, knowledge is constructed by doing, researching, and actively experiencing reality, rather than being the result of transmission. This assumes an intrinsic motivation of the student, who constructs knowledge by relating new information to existing knowledge.[22] Situated learning suggests that learning is a social activity, determined by the context in which learning takes place and the way in which groups of people share knowledge. Instead of acquiring abstract or context-free academic knowledge, students should develop knowledge that is linked to concrete applications, contexts, and cultures.[23]

Authentic learning is a representative of the social-constructivist learning approach. Roelofs and Houtveen[24] distinguish four principles of authentic learning:

a   Learning is connected to the student's personal world
    (aimed towards the culture of the student). It takes account
    of students' prior knowledge, providing space for students'
    opinions, nterests, and needs.
b   Learning is relevant to situations outside the school: learning
    tasks are derived from activities performed by professionals
    in society. A learning task is considered authentic when its
    origin and solution are accepted in the professional domain in
    which practitioners and experts are active.
c   Learning takes place in productive learning environments
    that are shaped by complex and complete task situations
    which give scope for students' initiative and exploration via
    divergent assignments, global guidelines, and global criteria.
    A productive learning environment is also aimed at the
    students' metacognitive processes.
d   Communication and cooperation play an important role
    in the learning process. Group tasks, student consultation,
    discussion presentations and (peer) evaluations are regular
    features of the learning process.

Authentic Arts Education

Authentic learning has also been applied to arts education.[25, 26]
Note that the adjective 'authentic' in Authentic Arts Education does
not refer to the arts, although some arts are called authentic, such
as historically informed music performances or visual art made with
traditional media. Nor does it apply to the modernist view that art
should be original and purely personal. In Authentic Arts Education,
'authenticity' refers to education and learning.

On the one hand, Authentic Arts Education tries to maintain a
relationship with the reality of students' everyday cultural experiences and practices that often are inspired by popular culture.
Authentic Arts Education acknowledges the students' personal
cultural preferences and interests as well as students' expertise
based on informal cultural production outside school. On the other
hand, Authentic Arts Education tries to provide a gateway into the
domain of present-day artistic production and contemporary socially
meaningful themes. It stimulates students to operate as artists
and critics, roles derived from the professional artworld. As such,
Authentic Arts Education can be considered the opposite of traditional school arts styles.

Universal Design for Learning

Background
Universal Design for Learning (UDL) was designed by the
Center for Applied Special Technology (Lynnfield, MA, USA).
Like Authentic Arts Education, it stands in the tradition of social
constructivism, but is complemented with recent insights on
learning and development in brain research.[27] At the heart of the
UDL-framework is the idea that learning should be made inclusive
and accessible to everyone.[28] While there is much variation among
students, according to UDL, a part of that variation is predictable
rather than random.[29] Therefore, UDL offers a framework for
designing a learning environment, which caters to a variety of
learners from the very beginning of curriculum development.
By catering to these differences, within a teacher's possibilities,
learning barriers can be dismantled as much as possible for *all*
students—and not just for one particular student—from the start
of any educational design trajectory.

Interestingly, the founders suggest that arts education and
UDL are a good match as 'arts offer rich, engaging, and meaningful
options for teaching and learning. These options provide alternative
pathways for addressing variability and enabling learners to find
their own directions for learning'.[30] They do, however, critically
note that—to be more inclusive and responsive to variety—arts
educators will have to be more sensitive to the differences between
their students. It is through recognizing their students' variation
in difficulties that arts educators can start addressing them. During
this process, educators can be challenged to expand their view of
who can be an artist and what we mean by 'art'.

The UDL-Framework
The UDL-framework is organized around three principles for curriculum design to help take into account variety and to consciously
make a learning experience accessible to more students. We will
shortly discuss these three principles.

Provide multiple means of engagement: the first design principle
is about generating and sustaining students' engagement. In
everyday classroom practice, (arts) teachers will recognize that
it is not easy to engage all students to learn—and often they will
be motivated in different ways. Yet, from an UDL perspective

engaging students is important to help them find a way into
a learning experience.[31]

Students' engagement can be enhanced by optimizing the
relevance of the learning content by presenting clear learning goals
and by creating assignments that connect to their prior knowledge,
(cultural) background, learning strategies, or their ability to collab-
orate.[32, 33] Another way is to optimize individual choice and autonomy
when it comes to choosing assignments, the work strategies, or materials students can work with. UDL also notes that teachers can
foster engagement through collaboration and community and, therefore, advises to work on (arts) assignments in a group when possible.

The ability to sustain motivation by learning to regulate
negative emotions and to persist working on an (arts) assignment
is also important. This asks teachers to provide emotional support
to their students and to help them to learn to persist.

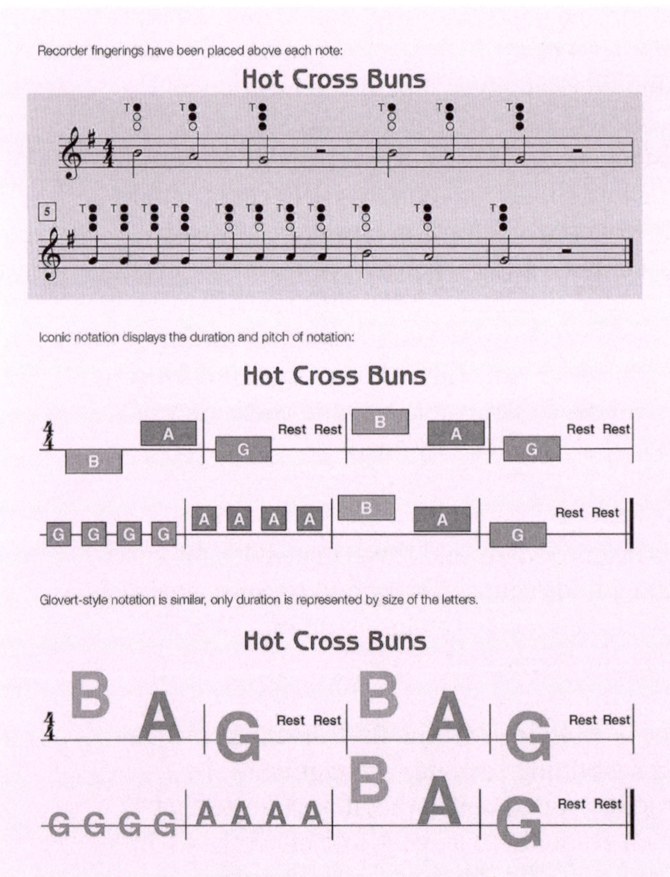

To give students different entry points to learning to play music, various musical notation systems could be offered[34]

Provide multiple means of representation: the second design principle of UDL concerns taking the different ways students perceive and process information into account.[35] Students' learning difficulties, language delays or sensory impairments (for instance, blindness, deafness, tactile deficiencies), all can impact on how they perceive and process information. Therefore, from a UDL perspective it is important to (re)present learning content in different ways, offering students multiple entry points to access the content.[36]

To provide multiple entry points, UDL challenges teachers to present content through multiple media and to think about how they can offer alternatives for both auditory and visual information. For instance, students might be allowed to choose between listening to a podcast, reading a book, or viewing a tutorial on the same (arts) topic. To provide multiple entry points for comprehending the content, teachers can demonstrate different working strategies, e.g. diverse strategies for practicing music, different ways to approach a writer's block, diverse strategies for observing and interpreting artworks (see music notation example left).

At a more practical level, UDL advises to take the speed or timing of video, animation or sound into account when presenting learning content, or to adjust the layout of visuals or other elements of learning content to students' needs. Teachers are also encouraged to support students' comprehension by connecting to prior knowledge, attracting attention to patterns, and guiding information processing and application.[37]

Provide multiple means of action and expression: the third design principle focuses on providing students with multiple means of action and expression, thus giving them the opportunity to express what they have learned in different ways.[38, 39] For example, if students with physical disabilities cannot write, they may still be able to make an audio recording, thereby showing what they have learned and know in a different way.

In the case of multiple means of actions, students should be allowed to approach an (arts) assignment in diverse ways, through the use of different materials, (arts) disciplines or working strategies. Looking at multiple means of expression, assignments should allow for diverse outcomes, providing a variety of ways in which students can express what they have made and learned.

Authentic Arts Education and UDL as the Basis for Wicked Arts Curricula

The five design principles of the model for Wicked Arts Curricula are based on Authentic Arts Education and UDL. In what follows, we will take a closer look at how these principles are rooted in those theories of learning.

Content
1. **Create connections between the domain of the _student_, the _arts_ and _society_ through themes and sources of inspiration**
2. **Provide a variety of meaningful materials and techniques**

One of the premises of Authentic Arts Education is that the relevance of education increases when it connects to three domains: the culture of the student, the arts, and society. Therefore, _Wicked Arts Education_ integrates a learner-, discipline-, and society-centred perspective on curriculum design in the same model. The inspirational sources from the three domains also provide multiple means of _representation_, offering multiple entry points for discussing and understanding the curriculum's theme.

Student _engagement_ is an important aspect of UDL and is enhanced through sources that specifically connect to the student's culture, prior knowledge, and interests. This engagement is also strengthened when artists from various disciplines, with different (cultural) backgrounds and genders to which students can relate are represented.

Lastly, through a variety of different materials and techniques, students are provided with multiple means of _action and expression_ to demonstrate what they have learned. From an authentic learning perspective, it is important that these materials and techniques are meaningful. This is achieved when students experience them not as typically 'school-like', but as 'art-like' or 'life-like'.

Pedagogy
3. **Design Wicked Arts Assignments based on enabling constraints**
4. **Address classes as learning communities, promoting various working strategies and expertise**

Wicked Arts Assignments are typically *holistic* and based on *enabling constraints*, which traces back to the social-constructivist principles that underpin both authentic learning and UDL. The assignments are *holistic* because they are not divided into small sub-tasks. Wicked Arts Assignments offer a midway between open and closed assignments because they are built on enabling constraints: a set of constraints that open possibilities by limiting choices (e.g. the use of certain materials or themes, or time limits).

The value of different working strategies and personal expertise is further underlined when the class is addressed as a learning community. Here the 'social learning' aspects of Authentic Arts Education and UDL are merged by defining a learning community as a collaborative environment in which diverse working strategies can be applied, and different forms of expertise of students and the teacher are shared.

Context
5. Provide opportunities for learning and assessment in lifelike contexts

Both from the perspective of Authentic Arts Education and UDL, the engagement of students is optimized when education becomes more relevant to them. A way to enhance engagement is to make students feel that learning and evaluation processes take place in lifelike contexts that offer opportunities for interaction with real participants or audiences.

Next Up: Backbone Curriculum

Now that you have been introduced to the model for Wicked Arts Curricula, get ready to start designing your Wicked Arts Curriculum yourselves! In the next chapter we will provide you with tools to creatively put the model and its design principles into practice.

NOTES

1   F. M. Newmann, H. M. Marks and
    A. Gamoran, 'Authentic Pedagogy
    and Student Performance', *American
    Journal of Education*, 104(4) (1996),
    pp. 280–312.
2   H. Gardner, *The Disciplined Mind:
    What All Students Should Understand*
    (Simon & Schuster, 1999).
3   A. Efland, 'The School Art Style:
    A Functional Analysis', *Studies in Art
    Education*, 17(2) (1976), p. 39.
4   L. Bresler, 'The Genre of School Music
    and its Shaping by Meso, Micro and
    Macro Contexts', *Research Studies in
    Music Education*, 11 (1998), pp. 2–18.
5   M. Bremmer and A. Huisingh, 'Music
    is When Sounds Come Together
    Nicely: Researching Preschool Music
    Education that is Based on the Image
    of the Competent Child', in S. Young
    and A.R. Adessi (eds.), *MERYC 2009:
    Proceedings of the 4th Conference
    of the European Network of Music
    Educators and Researchers of Young
    Children* (Bononia University Press,
    2009), pp. 295–302.
6   A. Efland, 'The School Art Style:
    A Functional Analysis', *Studies in Art
    Education*, 17(2), (1976), pp. 37–44.
7   L. Green, *'Meaning, Autonomy and
    Authenticity in the Music Classroom'*,
    inaugural professorial lecture (Institute
    of Education, London, 2005).
8   D. Atkinson, 'School Art Education:
    Mourning the Past and Opening a
    Future', *International Journal of Art &
    Design Education*, 25(1) (2006),
    pp. 16–27.
9   O. Gude, 'New School Art Styles:
    The Project of Art Education', *Art
    Education*, 66(1) (2013), pp. 6–15.
10 J. Harland, 'Voorstellen voor een even-
    wichtiger kunsteducatie' [Proposals
    for a More Balanced Arts Education]
    Cultuur+Educatie, 23 (2008), pp. 12–52.
11 Ibid., p. 47.
12 L. Vermeersch and W. Elias, "The End
    of the "To-Do-List"', in B. van Heusden
    and P. Gielen (eds.), A*rts Education
    Beyond Art: Teaching Art in Times of
    Change* (Valiz, 2015), pp. 113–130.
13 K. Arvedsen, F. Mathiesen and
    F. Billmayer, *Didaktik für das Fach
    Kunst* [Didactics for Art Education]
    (Fabrico Verlag, 2022).
14 T. Chong, 'Arts Education in Singapore:
    Between Rhetoric and Reality', *Journal
    of Social Issues in Southeast Asia*,
    32(1) (2017), pp. 107–136.
15 G. Cunha de Araujo, 'The Arts in
    Brazilian Public Schools: Analysis of
    an Art Education Experience in Mato
    Grosso State, Brazil', *Arts Education
    Policy Review*, 119(3) (2018), pp. 158–171.
16 M. R. Irwin, 'Arts Shoved Aside:
    Changing Art Practices in Primary
    Schools Since the Introduction of
    National Standards', *International
    Journal of Art & Design Education*,
    37(1) (2018), pp. 18–28.
17 T. IJdens and J. Lieven, 'Understan-
    dings of Arts Education', in T. IJdens,
    B. Bolden and E. Wagner (eds.),
    *Arts Education Around the World:
    International Yearbook for Research in
    Arts Education*, Vol. 5 (Waxmann, 2017).
18 B. Wilson, 'Of Diagrams and Rhizomes:
    Visual Culture, Contemporary Art,
    and the Impossibility of Mapping the
    Content of Art Education', *Studies in
    Art Education*, 44(3) (2003), p. 216.
19 Ibid., p. 225.
20 J. Steers, 'The Ever-Expanding Art
    Curriculum—Is It Teachable or
    Sustainable?', *International Journal
    of Education through Art*, 3(2)
    (2007), pp. 141–153.
21 J. Dewey, *The School and Society*
    (University of Chicago Press, 1907),
    p. 89.
22 E. C. Roelofs and J. Terwel, 'Const-
    ructivism and Authentic Pedagogy:
    State of the Art and Recent Develop-
    ments in the Dutch National Curri-
    culum in Secondary Education', *Journal
    of Curriculum Studies*, 31(2) (1999),
    pp. 201–227.
23 J. Lave and E. Wenger, *Situated
    Learning: Legitimate Peripheral
    Participation* (Cambridge University
    Press, 1991).

24 Roelofs and Houtveen, 'Didactiek van authentiek leren in de Basisvorming. Stand van zaken bij docenten Nederlands en wiskunde' [Didactics of Authentic Learning in Basic Education], *Pedagogische Studiën*, 76(4) (1999), pp. 237–257.

25 F. Haanstra, *'De Hollandse schoolkunst: mogelijkheden en beperkingen van authentieke kunsteducatie'* [The Dutch School Arts Style: Possibilities and Limitations of Authentic Art Education], oration (Cultuurnetwerk Nederland, 2001).

26 E. Heijnen, *Remixing the Art Curriculum: How Contemporary Visual Practices Inspire Authentic Art Education*, Ph.D. diss. (Radboud University Nijmegen, 2015).

27 A. Meyer, D. Rose and D. Gordon, *Universal Design for Learning: Theory and Practice* (CAST Professional Publishing, 2014).

28 F.R. Waitoller and K.A. King Thorius, 'Cross-Pollinating Culturally Sustaining Pedagogy and Universal Design for Learning: Toward an Inclusive Pedagogy that Accounts for Dis/ability', *Harvard Educational Review*, 86(3) (2016), pp. 366–389.

29 D. Glass, A. Meyer and D. H. Rose, 'Universal Design for Learning and the Arts', *Harvard Educational Review*, 83(1) (2013), pp. 98–119.

30 Ibid., p. 107.

31 Meyer, Rose and Gordon, *Universal Design for Learning*.

32 Glass, Meyer and Rose, 'Universal Design for Learning and the Arts'.

33 L. Lord Nelson, *Design and Deliver Planning and Teaching Using Universal Design for Learning* (Paul Brookes Publishing, 2014).

34 K. McCord, A. Gruben and J. Rathgeber, *Accessing Music: Enhancing Student Learning in the General Music Classroom Using UDL* (Alfred Music, 2014).

35 Lord Nelson, *Design and Deliver Planning and Teaching Using Universal Design for Learning*.

36 Meyer, Rose and Gordon, *Universal Design for Learning*.

37 Glass, Meyer and Rose, 'Universal Design for Learning and the Arts'.

38 Lord Nelson, *Design and Deliver Planning and Teaching Using Universal Design for Learning*.

39 Meyer, Rose and Gordon, *Universal Design for Learning*.

Chapter 3

Backbone Curriculum

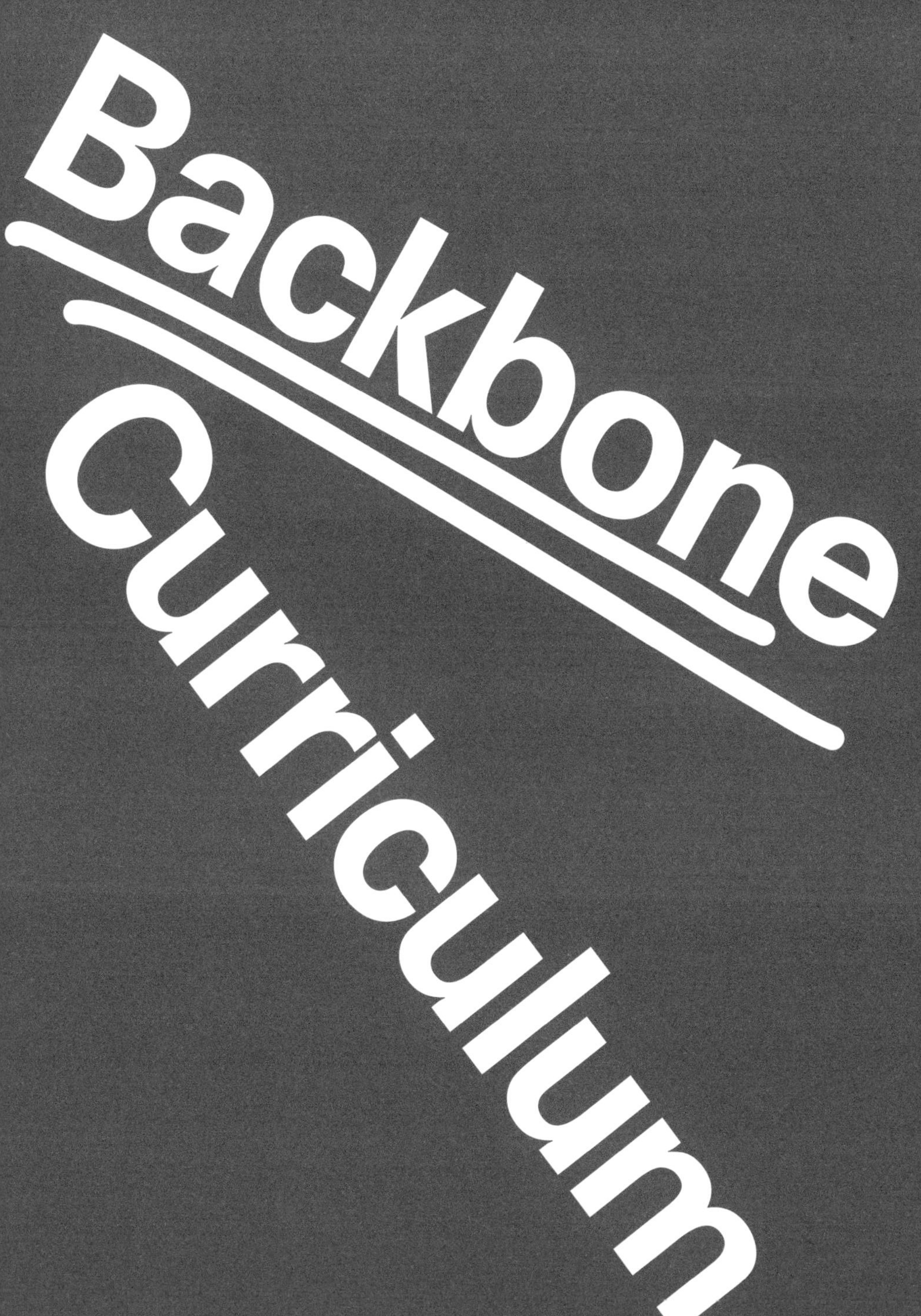

Slapdash Supercars is a series of artistic interventions by Namibian-German artist Max Siedentopf. Roaming the streets at night, he transforms ordinary cars in a slapdash way with his custom-made cardboard accessories that include fenders, wraps, spoilers, and exhausts. After photographing the upgraded cars, Siedentopf quickly removes the add-ons, returning the cars to their original state. How Siedentopf goes about this is actually exemplary for the phase of designing your backbone curriculum. Just as Siedentopf, you and your co-designers can create an image of what is possible and let your creativity flow. In this phase, you will make a first, quick intuitive design of your curriculum. Permit yourself to enjoy that ride!

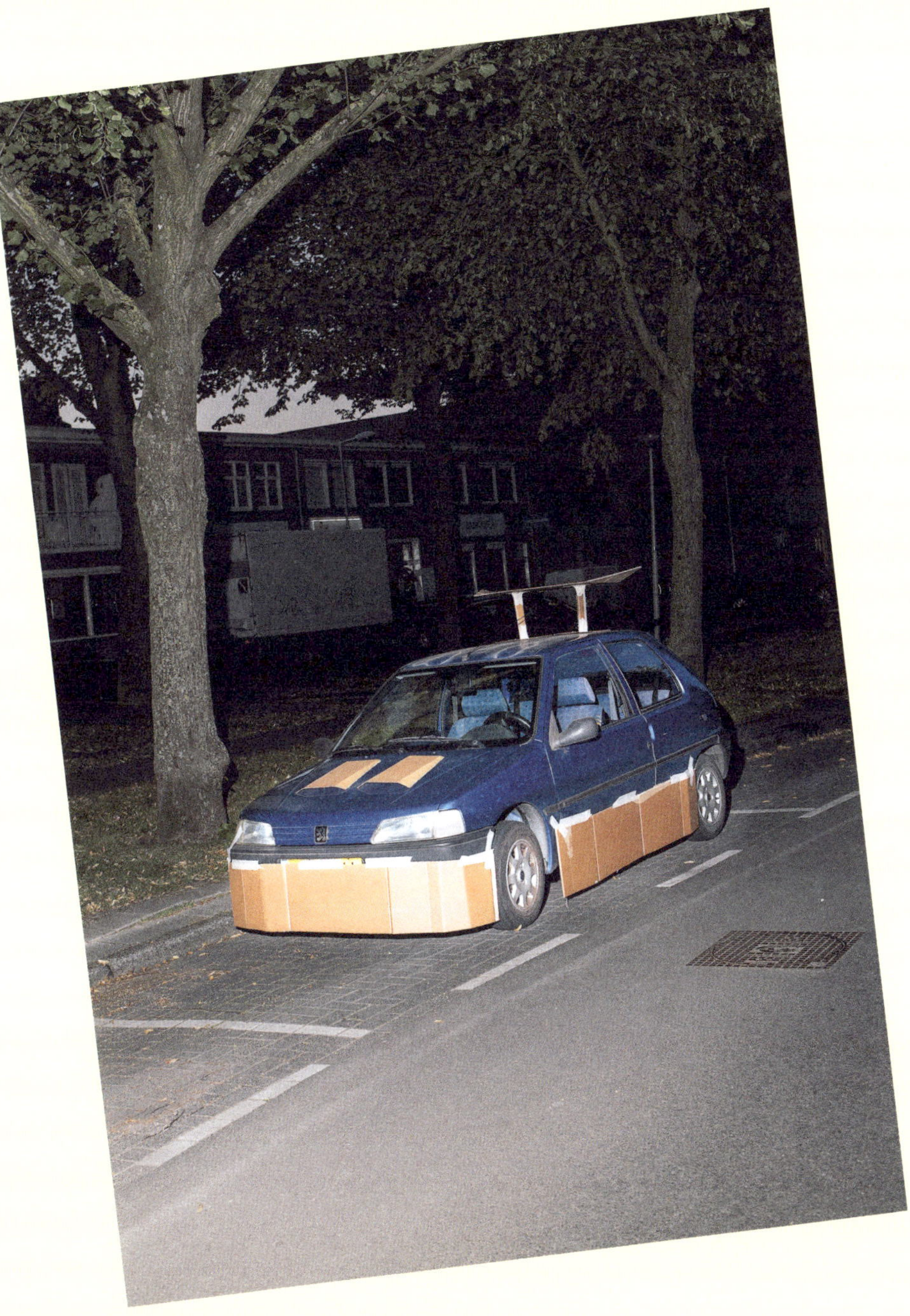

Max Siedentopf, *Slapdash Supercars* (2015)

Contents of this chapter

3.1 Backbone Curriculum

Although curriculum design is often presented as a systematic process that starts with learning goals and ends with evaluation,[1] the reality is much messier. Systematically collected learning goals, criteria, content matter, methods, and media, do not necessarily make an inspiring course design. Therefore, we agree with Eisner and Earl that instructional design processes cannot be based on logical thinking alone, but need creativity and intuition.[2,3] A way to 'invite' creativity in, is to start the design process with a compact and holistic overview of your curriculum: a backbone curriculum. Backbone curriculum design means that you sketch the core components of your curriculum upon which the rest is built. In a limited amount of time, you will design your curriculum in a nutshell, which you can systematically develop further during the later phases of the design process (see chapters 4–8). Because the backbone curriculum design process is open and benefits from different expertises and ideas, it is especially suitable for collaborative curriculum design.

We propose three different design strategies for your backbone curriculum. Importantly, these strategies provide you with tools to put the design principles of the model for a Wicked Arts Curriculum into practice. Every time you design a lesson, project, or course, you and your co-designers can choose which one of these strategies suits the design process best. You may want to start designing from a collection of sources, a single artwork may deliver the ultimate curriculum-spark, or you may want to construct your Wicked Arts Assignment first. In all cases, these design strategies will give you a head start to complete your backbone curriculum, the basis for the other design phases of your curriculum.

A complete backbone curriculum offers an overview of the main inspirational sources, 'Responsive Environment Organizer(s)' and the theme you will use in the curriculum. Furthermore, it will consist of the central Wicked Arts Assignment(s), the key materials and techniques, and the physical and social contexts in which the curriculum is implemented.

T To help you and your colleagues along with the design process,
I you can use the online or printed version (page 183) of the model
P for a Wicked Arts Curriculum. By working with the model, you
will gain a visual overview of your backbone curriculum and at
a glance you will see how your sources, assignment, and materials
are related during the whole educational design process.

3.2 Inspirational Sources from the Three Domains

A powerful way to start the creative process of designing is to use sources of inspiration from the three domains (student, arts, and society) of the model for a Wicked Arts Curriculum. From a collection of various sources a central curriculum theme or Wicked Arts Assignment can emerge. For instance, we were intrigued by the phenomenon of catfishing, the practice of making a fake online profile to trick people (the domain of society). That led us to search for other related sources ranging from the Superman superhero comics (the domain of the student) to the self-portraits of Cindy Sherman, where she depicts herself as various imagined characters (the domain of the arts). From these sources, the theme 'alter ego' emerged, leading to the Wicked Arts Assignment 'Photograph your alter ego in a fitting environment.'

Discussing different sources provides students with different entry points for understanding the main theme and the Wicked Arts Assignment of your curriculum. Each source may be selected for its capacity to deepen the theme, to motivate the student, or to stimulate critical and creative thinking. Hence, a selection of varied sources as content matter reinforces connections between the students' culture, societal themes, and the professional arts.[4] Therefore, your backbone curriculum will generally include at least three inspirational sources, one for each domain.

Three Domains Design Strategy

By selecting at least three sources for your lesson or project, you are challenged to find ones that highlight the same theme from three different angles. The trick here is to select three sources that have a logical thematic connection. Selecting three random sources will not provide you with a clear, overarching theme. Disney's *Snow White* (student), Frida Kahlo's *Self-Portrait with Thorn Necklace and Hummingbird* (arts), and Al Gore's *An Inconvenient Truth* (society) do not seem to have much in common. However, when the societal source is replaced by Sean Illing's book *How the West Became a Self-obsessed Culture*, themes like 'selfies' or 'self-perception' emerge.

Wicked Arts Education

To work with this design strategy, you and your team can use the model for a Wicked Arts Curriculum. A good way to start is to place a source that you want to include in your lesson in the corresponding domain-circle. Then you start brainstorming about which sources from the other domains could match that source. Feel free to add different sources during this phase of the process, stay in the flow, and avoid premature decisions about the sources.

When several sources have been added, see which three sources form an overarching theme. Having established this, the three sources and the theme form the basis for the formulation of the Wicked Arts Assignment (see design strategy 2.4) and the other aspects of your backbone curriculum, such as learning goals and activities. For example, a lesson series about court culture (society) of the Italian renaissance (arts) gets a seductive contemporary entry point when the realistic adventure video game *Assassin's Creed* (student) is added to the content matter (see figure below).

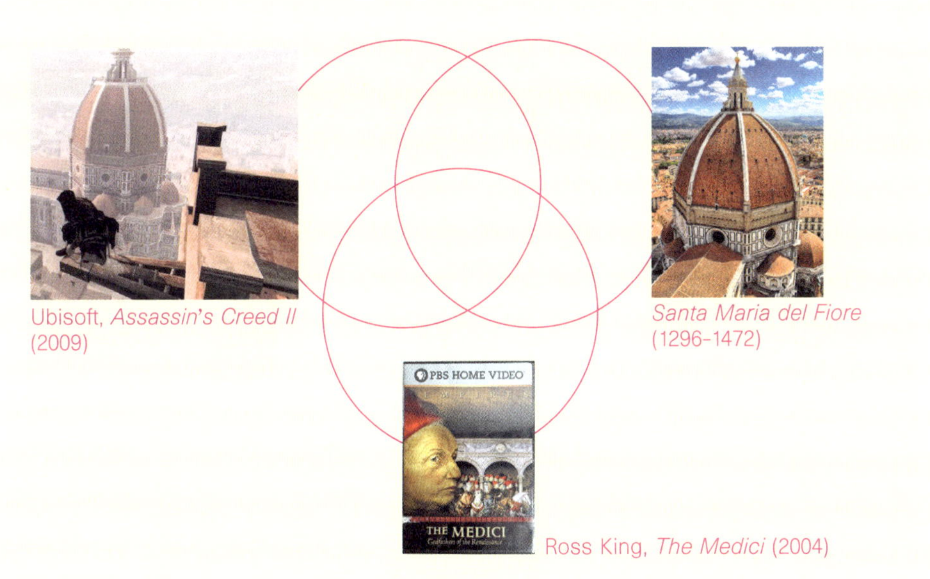

Components of a lesson series about court culture of the Italian Renaissance

Another strategy is to start brainstorming with only one given source, belonging to one of the three domains. The design-question is now what sources from other domains can complement this piece of content, and what theme might emerge. This process is illustrated in the example *The Tractor Dilemma.*

The Tractor Dilemma

This concept for a lesson series originated during a curriculum design workshop. A group of teachers from a secondary school in a rural region wondered how they could motivate local boys for arts education, because 'the only content matter they are interested in are farming tractors'. We decided to frame this 'problem' as a curriculum opportunity, and took a picture of a tractor as the starting point of the lesson design process. During the following brainstorm the work *V12 Laraki* by Algerian-Belgian artist Éric Van Hove popped up. The Laraki is the first car ever designed and manufactured in Morocco. Only its engine is German-made, a Mercedes 6.0L V12. To make the Laraki symbolically 100% local, Van Hove had an imported engine block reproduced in an ornamental style by 42 Moroccan master craftsmen. Van Hove's practice deals with questions around the role of craft and design in a globalized society, which helped the teachers decide that 'craft' and 'local communities' could be the main subjects of the societal domain. When the term 'pimping' was added, the Wicked Arts Assignment presented itself almost automatically to the design team: transform a farming vehicle into a local hipster ride.

Assignment:
Transform a farming vehicle into a local hipster ride

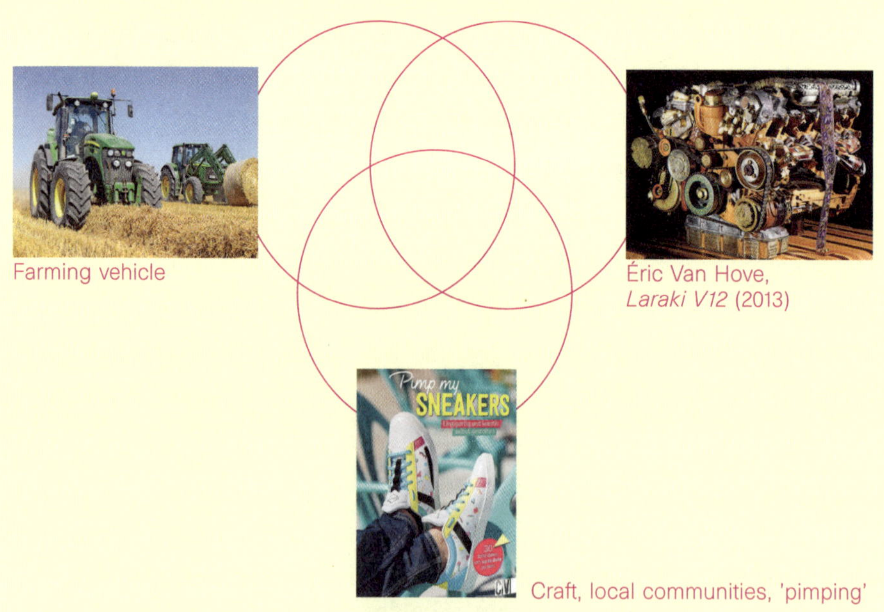

Farming vehicle

Éric Van Hove,
Laraki V12 (2013)

Craft, local communities, 'pimping'

Components of a lesson series around the assignment *Transform a farming vehicle into a local hipster ride*

3.3 Responsive Environment Organizer

Interestingly, some sources, for instance contemporary artworks, have the capacity to address all three domains at the same time. Such 'super-sources' are called Responsive Environment Organizers (REO).[5] A well-chosen REO can help to formulate the theme and Wicked Arts Assignment of a project or lesson. As many arts educators know, artworks embody ideas, theories, processes, and opinions that can inspire you to articulate a course's central theme. Similarly, music educator Wiggins[6] noted that finding a good piece of music 'can make a lesson almost plan itself'.

A REO that addresses all three domains, such as a contemporary film, music video, or play, can also have a pedagogical function for students. It can act as a strong anchor for them—a work they can return to, one that exemplifies what is possible and what has already been done. Whilst introducing and discussing such REOs with students, we believe that arts educators should not be tempted to reduce artworks to a few simple formal features that can be easily applied, copied, and remixed in their own work. Rather, students should encounter their complexity: artworks can confront, tell compelling stories, show new truths, elicit strong emotions, or transport you to other realities.[7] Furthermore, by observing the way artists use techniques and materials in their work, students can also acquire artistic clues as to how to approach their own creative process.

REO Design Strategy

At the beginning of your design process, you can start your work from a chosen REO; you can choose any artwork; one that intrigues, annoys, or surprises you. Note what you believe the artwork is telling you: what themes, opinions or ideas does the work of art open? Next step is to formulate a Wicked Arts Assignment based on what the artwork is communicating. In this phase, failing is an option, self-censorship is not! Allow yourself and your co-designers to enjoy the creative process of writing down as many assignments as possible. Out of the different Wicked Arts Assignments you can choose and refine the one that is the most fitting for your lesson, project, or course. Here is an example of how a single artwork by M.I.A. generated different assignments during collective design sessions with arts educators.

**Example REO (Responsive Environment Organizer):
M.I.A., *Bad Girls* (2012)**

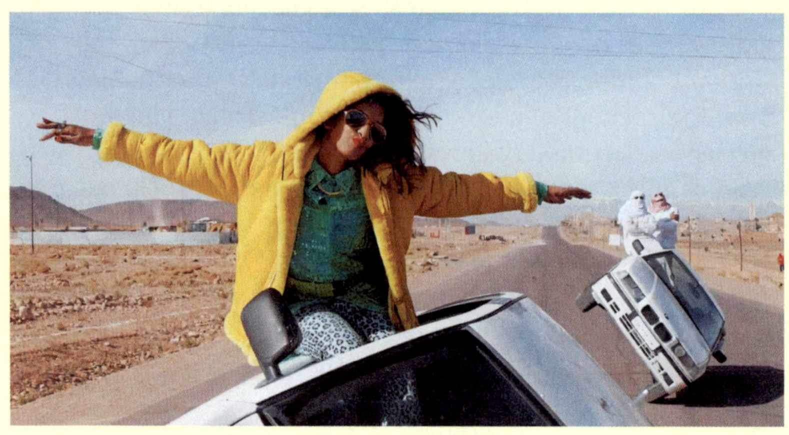

M.I.A., *Bad Girls* (2012), video still

Rapper and singer M.I.A (Maya Arulpragasam) grew up in Sri Lanka, India, and England and integrates musical influences from all over the world into her music. Her music video *Bad Girls* was shot in the North African desert and is packed with thrilling car stunts, including driving on two wheels and people 'skating' on the sun-baked tarmac while hanging out of a speeding car. M.I.A. and director Romain Gavras were inspired by an encounter with a female truck driver in Iran and the videos they discovered online with Arab youth doing unbelievable stunts with their parents' cars. As a 'lady gangsta fantasy', *Bad Girls* celebrates various hip hop clichés, such as tough protagonists, gun waving, pimped cars, and outrageous outfits, but in a much less stereotypical Arabic context. Journalist Dina Dabbous of Al Bawaba states that M.I.A. turns the oriental fantasy on its head, being 'not afraid to trash social graces as well as smash gender or racial stereotypes'.[8] The analysis of *Bad Girls* generated different Wicked Arts Assignments, such as:

- **Make an artwork that celebrates an underground trend**
- **Make a choreography with a vehicle**
- **Compose a new piece of music by remixing three different musical styles**
- **Make a fashion statement that empowers an under-represented group**
- **Make a theatre scene in which a bad reputation is turned into a good one**

3.4 Wicked Arts Assignment

The heart of your backbone curriculum is a central Wicked Arts Assignment, the focal point of your lessons. A major question is how you can design a Wicked Arts Assignment that will unleash the creativity of your students. When arts assignments are formulated very tightly, focusing on the execution of 'step by step' instructions, students often produce highly comparable and uninspired outcomes.[9] At the opposite end: if they are given huge amounts of freedom, students seem paralyzed by it, and simply do not know how to begin working on an assignment, or produce predictable results.[10] In that same vein, Sawyer notes that *un*constrained assignments tend to result in less creative outcomes.[11]

We believe there is a midway for highly constrained or fully unconstrained arts assignments. Davis and Sumara coined the idea of 'enabling constraints'.[12] They explain that enabling constraints function as a set of rules, like those of a game: *because* rules of a game limit how it can be played, the game can unfold in endless different ways. In other words, by narrowing down students' choices through constraints this paradoxically opens possibilities for them. Therefore, if chosen well, constraints can provide students with some direction for their creative process without prescribing an end product.

Wicked Arts Assignment Design Strategy

In our practice, we have found that if arts educators compress an assignment into a short sentence, it turns into an 'anchor' for students: a powerful sentence that can explain an assignment by itself, and that helps them to connect additional explanations and demands back to the assignment.[13]

A useful strategy to formulate a compact Wicked Arts Assignment is to address the student directly, by starting the assignment with a verb such as 'make, choreograph, design, compose, build, create, write, perform or produce' (see also Richard Serra's verb list in chapter 4). Make sure your sentence is not too long—your students should be able to understand the assignment immediately and to memorize it!

Wicked Arts Assignments will also contain one or more enabling constraints, which may refer to the content, or materials and techniques students must work with. To give you an idea of possible constraints you could use we will discuss a few, but must stress that the choice of constraints is endless.

Themes

Themes themselves can function as inspiring constraints for Wicked Arts Assignments. They can range from more playful ones such as superheroes to more socially engaged themes, for instance, sustainability. A thematic approach also provides opportunities to establish connections with non-arts disciplines and for students to develop cross-curricular skills.

Example: *Make a data visualization based on a review of your debts* (after Heath Schultz, 2023).

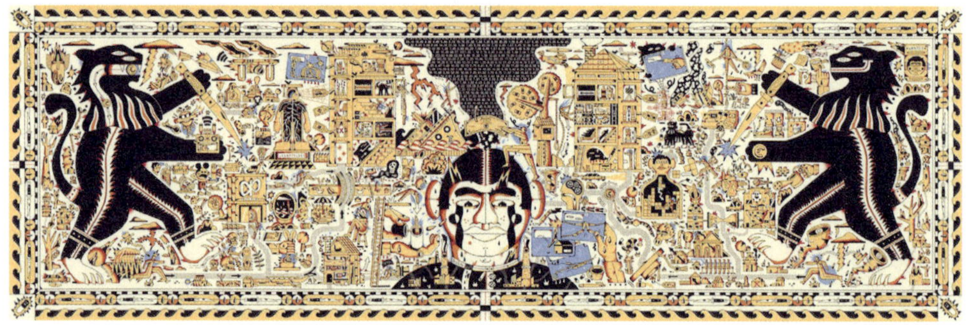

Mart Veldhuis, *Eigen Schuld* (2021). When Veldhuis graduated from arts school, he visualized his student debt of € 45,879.40 in the form of a 470 × 150 cm tapestry. In 2023, the work was sold for exactly that amount. The title *Eigen Schuld* is a play on words that can either mean 'your debt' or 'your fault'

Interdisciplinarity

Challenging students to work with more than one arts discipline can also be a fruitful constraint. Students may be asked to make a choreography based on a painting, to design a visual poem inspired by lyrics, or to make a score for a film. A particular discipline might be an inspiration for an artwork in a different discipline, or students may be asked to integrate arts disciplines.

Example: *Photograph something you are touched by and turn it into a musical performance or drag show* (Eva Custers, Maarten Tas, 2023).

Target group

Another constraint is the target group students have to make something for. This invites students to take the perspective of a group of people and to make something that is suited to that group.

Example: *Ring at the doorbell of no. 8 and make a work for its residents* (anonymous, 2017).

Materials/techniques

Constraints can be used to limit the materials or techniques students must work with. Students can be moved out of their creative comfort zone if the materials challenge them to work in different ways. They might only be allowed to work with intangible materials such as certain music notes or particular words, or tangible materials such as Lego, particular (digital) instruments, or tap dance shoes.

Example: *Make a still life using only Cheetos corn crisps* (Ryan Bulis, 2023).

Time

Constraints may also relate to the working process of arts production, like when 'time' is used as a limitation in an assignment. Students might be asked to produce a work of art that should only last one minute, or to photograph their pet for a whole week, a month or a year.

Example: *Create a one-minute composition with only computer-generated sounds from across the world in 2050* (Allerd van den Bremen, 2024).

Collaboration

Another constraint has to do with collaboration. You can decide the number of collaborative partners students have to work with, including people from outside the school. Or one student or class may start producing a work that another student or class has to finish.

Example: *Make up a rumour about this school and make sure the parallel class believes this gossip and can retell it vividly* (Sjoerd Wintzen, 2023).

3.5. Additional Design Considerations

After you have decided on your inspirational sources or a REO, and your central Wicked Arts Assignment, there are still some design considerations left that should be taken into account.

Provocative Questions

During a course or project, teachers can help students to explore the theme of the inspirational sources, REO or Wicked Arts Assignment. By instigating a discussion on a theme, students can encounter multiple perspectives and are invited to deepen, broaden, or rethink their own perspective on it.[14] Through speaking and listening to one another, they can also be provoked to develop a critical stance on a theme that plays a role in their own life, the arts, and society. Furthermore, talking about a theme in depth, may stimulate students to explore and generate ideas for their own artwork, thus inspiring their subsequent creative process.[15]

Design consideration: for your backbone curriculum, formulate 'provocative questions' that accompany the theme of the inspirational sources, REO or Wicked Arts Assignment. Generally, provocative questions are open-ended questions that are not meant to elicit black or white answers, but encourage students to engage in and critically explore a theme.

Examples of Provocative Questions

Theme: disability in the arts

Questions at secondary level:
- What do equality and equity mean to you?
- What physical, sensory, cognitive, or communication barriers exist in the arts?
- Why does society label certain human differences as a disability?
- What issues do you think disability rights groups campaign for?
- In what ways can society be more inclusive of people with disabilities?

Provocative questions: disability in the arts

Materials and Techniques

Artists and designers illustrate that hands-on working and thinking do not form a contradiction, but reinforce each other during creative processes. Or, as sociologist Sennett puts it: 'making is thinking'.[16] Similarly, the designer Ratto observes that one can critically think through the process of making—and therefore prefers to talk about 'critical making'.[17] The materials and techniques that artists or students work with, therefore, matter.

The use of specific materials and techniques, such as sensors, paint, tap dance or playing pizzicato, can have a profound effect on a creative process: often students will let go of their initial concept, simply because materials did not 'do' what they wanted them to do or gave rise to alternative ideas.[18] As such, an artistic process revolves around the confrontation with material, tools, props, and instruments, and does not automatically run in a straight line from a concept to its realization. Furthermore, by simultaneously producing, assessing, and judging works of art, students can be stimulated to make/think critically about the world.[19]

Design consideration: as we mentioned earlier, the school arts style tends to make use of easily manipulated materials that can be cleaned or cleared away easily, such as crayons or boomwhackers. In contrast, in *Wicked Arts Education* materials and techniques will ideally relate to the professional artworld and provide students with a variety of materials and techniques to work with. As curriculum designers, you can turn to your sources of inspiration or your assignment when thinking about what materials and techniques you could use in your lessons. What ways of working, techniques, and materials do they demonstrate? Your backbone curriculum will include a short description of what materials you feel are necessary for students to work with and the techniques you would like them to learn.

Physical and Social Contexts

The physical and social contexts in which artworks are produced matter, and from the viewpoint of *Wicked Arts Education* this also applies to the contexts in which art is learned. Looking at the physical context, learning becomes more authentic when the educational environment is as little school-like as possible. This can be achieved by offering students a realistic learning environment that includes 'arts-like' spaces, materials and interactions with arts professionals. You might try to realize this ideal in your institution, but sometimes a more effective solution is to simply move lessons to a space other than the school. The presentation of your students' rap battles is a little more lifelike in the town park than in the school's hall.

Regarding the social context, take into account that there are other models than the artist as the lone genius who works in isolation. Many contemporary artists work in collectives or deliberately seek the unpredictable social interaction in neighbourhoods or public space as artistic contexts.[20] The artist William Kentridge also notes that by walking around in an atelier or theatre artists are not only confronted with materials but also with other bodies that spur their creative process.[21]

Design consideration: for your backbone curriculum, think about the space where the curriculum will be implemented and the social interactions you want your students to engage in. During this process, your sources of inspiration may inspire you. Where and with whom are such artworks typically made? In an atelier, studio, theatre, music hall, on the Internet, or on location? With a specific group of people?

T   Lesson series *Imagine...*
I   is an example of a complete
P   backbone curriculum.

Lesson series *Imagine...*

Assignment:
Design an interactive installation in which participants can experience neurodiversity or a disability

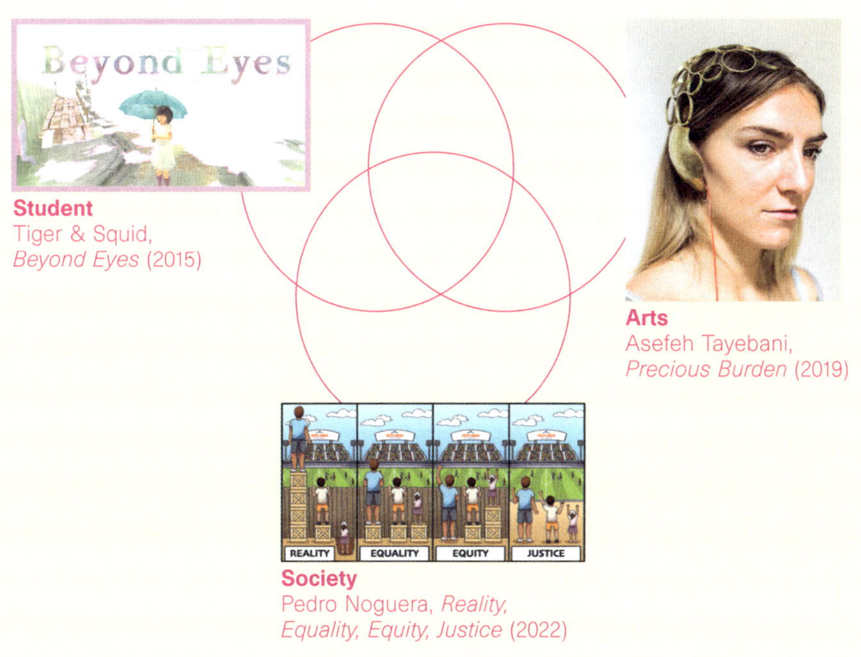

Student
Tiger & Squid,
Beyond Eyes (2015)

Arts
Asefeh Tayebani,
Precious Burden (2019)

Society
Pedro Noguera, *Reality,
Equality, Equity, Justice* (2022)

Provocative Questions	**Materials and Techniques**	**Physical and Social Contexts**
• What do equality and equity mean to you? • Why does society label certain human differences as a 'disability'? • In what ways can society be more inclusive of people with disabilities?	• 2D/3D: Construction tools and supplies, painting tools and supplies. • Audiovisual: cameras, screens, software for image, sound and interactive design, electronic STEAM kits.	• Students work in the school's Maker Space, the layout of which is derived from professional workshops. • During the working process, students receive feedback from experience experts.

Backbone curriculum example of the lesson series *Imagine...*

The lesson series *Imagine...* was inspired by the REO *Precious Burden* by designer Asefeh Tayebani. With the wearables collection *Precious Burden*, Tayebani playfully evokes compassion and understanding for people with autism. The different wearables let you feel how autistic people process stimuli in daily life. For instance, a golden sleeve designed to be worn on your arm employs sensors and subtle electric shocks to simulate a heightened sensitivity to touch. Additionally, a head-worn jewel amplifies and distorts incoming sounds, utilizing a microphone on your chest to replicate the auditory challenges faced by those with autism.

The wearable collection *Precious Burden* demarks 'dealing with human differences' as the central theme for a lesson series. This theme is broadened by a source that relates to the culture of the student. In the video game *Beyond Eyes* by Tiger & Squid (2015) you play as Rae—a blind girl leaving the safety of her garden to search for her lost feline friend. The societal domain is represented by theoretical sources that discuss concepts such as disability justice and equity.

The central assignment of this course is: *Develop an interactive installation in which participants can experience neurodiversity or a disability*, with underlying provocative questions that are related to equality and equity in contemporary society. Working in small groups, students first choose a 'human difference' that they want to explore further. Subsequently, they design an innovative interactive installation that gives others a convincing experience of the chosen difference.

3.6 Design Result: Your Curriculum in a Nutshell

For your backbone curriculum you will have designed or decided on the following:

- inspirational sources in the domains of the student, the arts and society, connected by a theme (or one or more REO's, addressing the three domains and theme);
- a central Wicked Arts Assignment;
- provocative questions that help students to explore and discuss the underlying key theme, ideas or concepts;
- the materials and techniques for students to work with;
- the physical and social context where students work at and the people they interact with.

Next Up: Learning Goals

In the following chapters we will look at how you can develop your backbone curriculum into a detailed curriculum, in a more systematic and analytical way. We discuss the design of learning goals, the structuring of learning content, the design of learning activities, and how you can assess your students' work. Although these design phases are presented in a linear way, it is worthwhile to keep in mind that in practice these phases are messier. Probably, you will navigate different design phases: if you change one element in a certain phase of your design, this will also have an effect on the other phases, which then might need changing. However, in the end it is important that all phases are aligned and form a coherent curriculum.

NOTES

1   R. W. Tyler, *Basic Principles of Curriculum and Instruction* (University of Chicago Press, 1949).

2   E. W. Eisner, *The Educational Imagination: On the Design and Evaluation of School Programs* (Macmillan, 1979).

3   T. Earl, *The Art and Craft of Course Design* (Kogan Page Ltd, 1987).

4   E. Heijnen, H. Braam and C. van Tongeren, 'Bring Fake News into the World: A Lesson Study Based on the Principles of Authentic Art Education', *Visual Arts Research*, 47(2) (2021), pp. 22-40.

5   T. Earl, op. cit., p. 103.

6   J. Wiggins, *Teaching for Musical Understanding* (Oxford University Press, 2014), p. 61.

7   G. Biesta, *Letting Art Teach* (ArtEZ Press, 2021).

8   D. Dabbous, 'In Defense of MIA's "Bad Girl" Arab-bashing', *Albawaba* (February 11th, 2012).

9   M. Bremmer and E. Heijnen, 'Bridging Contradictions: The Design of Wicked Arts Assignments', E. Heijnen and M. Bremmer (eds.), *Wicked Arts Assignments* (Valiz, 2020), pp. 23-32.

10   E. Winner, An *Uneasy Guest in the Schoolhouse: Art Education from Colonial Times to a Promising Future* (Oxford University Press, 2022).

11   R. K. Sawyer, 'Teaching and Learning How to Create in Schools of Art and Design', *Journal of the Learning Sciences*, 27(1) (2018), pp. 137-181.

12   B. Davis and D. Sumara, "If things were simple...': Complexity in Education', *Journal of Evaluation in Clinical Practice*, 16(4) (2010), pp. 856-860.

13   E. Heijnen, *Remixing the Art Curriculum: How Contemporary Visual Practices Inspire Authentic Art Education*, Ph.D. diss. (Radboud University Nijmegen, 2015).

14   P. Gardiner, 'Learning to Think Together: Creativity, Interdisciplinary Collaboration and Epistemic Control', *Thinking Skills and Creativity*, 38 (2020), 100749.

15   C. Ishiguro and T. Okad, 'How Does Art Viewing Inspire Creativity?', *The Journal of Creative Behavior*, 55(3) (2020), pp. 489-500.

16   R. Sennett, *The Craftsman* (Allen Lane, 2008), p. 10.

17   M. Ratto, 'Critical Making: Conceptual and Material Studies in Technology and Social Life', *The Information Society: An International Journal*, 27(4) (2011), pp. 252-260.

18   I. Buurke and V. Van 't Hoogt, 'Curious hands: maken en leren maken' [Curious Hands: Making and Learning to Make] *Cultuur + educatie*, 19(54) (2020), pp. 46-63.

19   C. F. Quigley and D. Herro, '"Finding the joy in the unknown": Implementation of STEAM Teaching Practices in Middle School Science and Math Classrooms', *Journal of Science Education and Technology*, 25(3) (2016), pp. 410-426.

20   Heijnen, *Remixing the Art Curriculum*.

21   W. Kentridge, *Six Drawing Lessons: The Charles Eliot Norton Lectures, 2012* (Harvard University Press, 2014).

Learning Goals

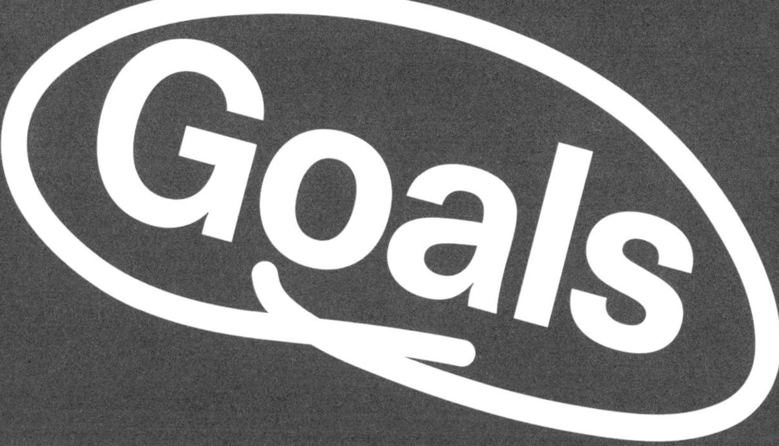

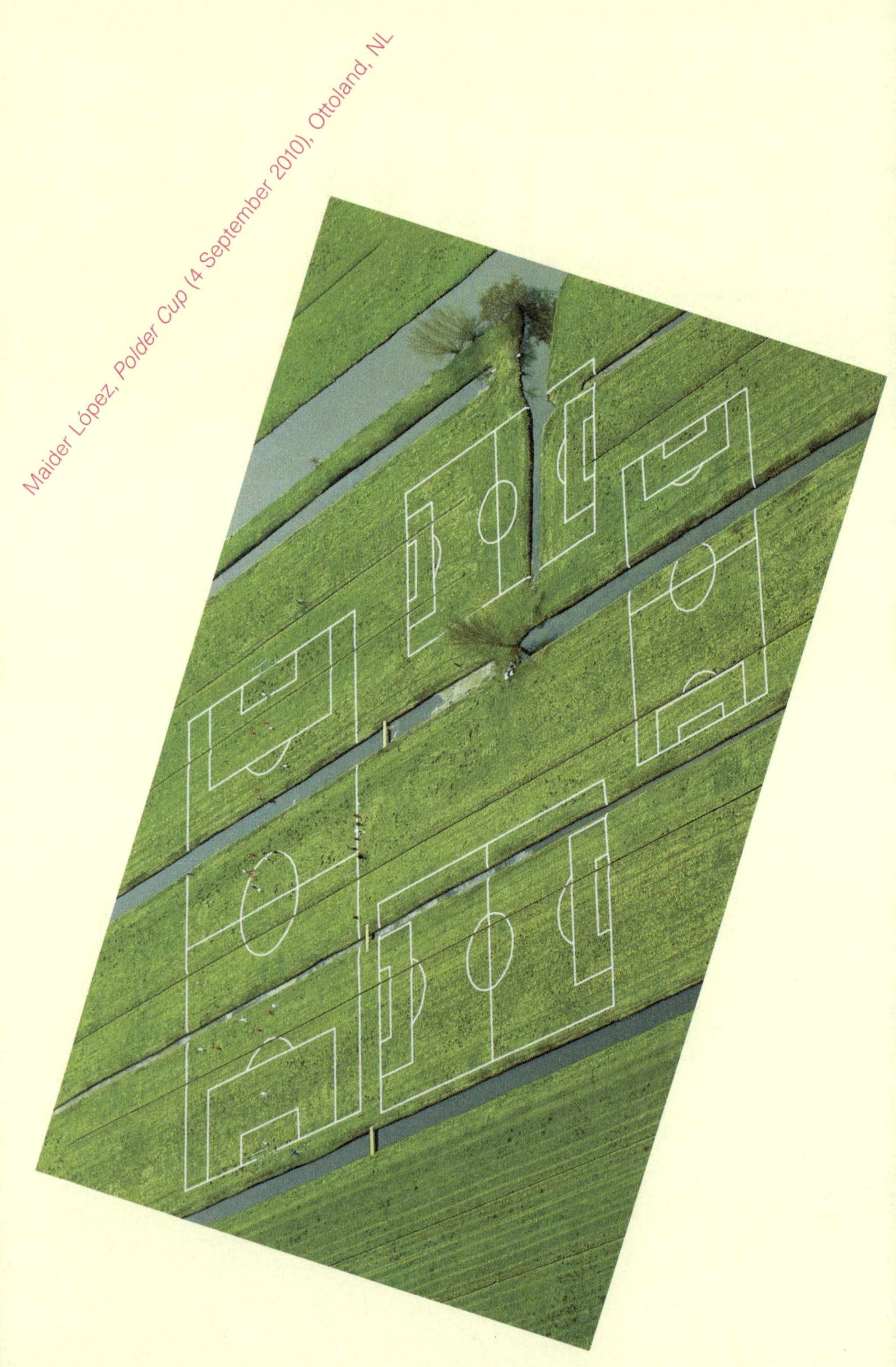

In *Polder Cup*, the Spanish artist Maider López organized a one-day soccer championship in the Dutch polders. She placed the soccer fields in such a way that water channels intersected them. In these new playing fields, the long grass, pollen, and spongy ground complicated the players' movements. All of a sudden, they had to change their playing tactics and develop new strategies to be able to reach their goal of scoring.

For arts teachers, the mere idea of learning goals can give rise to negative feelings: they may feel that they stifle their students' creativity. Yet, we believe that goals can give direction to a curriculum, but still leave space for students to play around and find ways to reach those goals. So be as Maider López—and start developing a challenging learning field for your students to playfully navigate.

Contents of this chapter

4.1 Imagine Your Ideal Curriculum

Just sit down for a moment. Take a deep breath, feel the soles of your feet, and relax. Are you sitting comfortably? Yes? Look at your backbone curriculum. Then start imagining vividly what the last day of your arts educational project or course would look like and what your students would have achieved by then.[1] See in your mind's eye what your students learned during the arts educational project through the process of experimenting, making, presenting, and critically reflecting on their work and that of others:[2]

- What artistic skills and techniques have students developed?
- How were students engaged in their work, and were they able to persist working on their piece of art, even when they felt frustrated?
- What theoretical (arts) concepts have students learned and applied?
- What types of works have students developed? With what kind of materials, instruments, technology, or props?
- How have students presented their work?
- How have students learned to conceptualize and discuss their work?
- How have students deepened their own knowledge and skills, their knowledge on the arts and on broader societal themes?

Write down freely what your students should have achieved, in any random order and without too much conscious thought. What you see written down reflects your ideal curriculum. It is what students can do under the perfect circumstances, without time constraints, and with a manifold of materials or instruments.

Yet, when designing a curriculum for a real-life context you often must consider time and resource constraints and cater to many different learners. Now begins the active transformation of your imagined curriculum into learning goals for a curriculum that fits the reality of the classroom, but still holds the essence of your ideal. In this transformational process, remembering why you work with learning goals and how you can formulate them can be very useful.

4.2 Learning Goals

Why Work with Learning Goals?

You might be surprised, but learning goals have much to offer both students and teachers.[3] From the perspective of the student, in general learning goals can function as a safeguard for equality. If formulated in an inclusive way, you will be able to ensure that students with all kinds of backgrounds will attain certain knowledge and skills (see paragraph 3.3). But learning goals have more to offer students. By making them explicit at the beginning of a lesson, course, or project, they can function as an advanced organizer: similar to a trailer of a new, exciting TV series, learning goals can provide students with a preview of what is coming.[4] Concepts and topics in learning goals can also activate students' prior knowledge, facilitating the integration of already acquired knowledge and skills with new knowledge and skills.[5] Learning goals can also give students a clear picture of what is expected of them. This in turn can help them to direct and monitor their learning throughout the course or project by referring back to the learning goals.[6]

From the perspective of arts educators, the process of formulating learning goals enables you to really think about which content, materials and learning activities are the most important for your students within the time and space of a curriculum. It challenges you to make creative choices about what should go in a curriculum, but also which pieces of content or learning activities can be left out, even though in themselves they might be gems. Learning goals, then, serve as a guide for further designing, adapting, and elaborating your curriculum. Lastly, learning goals also serve another important purpose: they form the basis for the design of learning activities (see chapter 6) and for the assessment of students' learning (see chapter 7).

Formulating Learning Goals

Richard Serra, *Verb List* (1967)

When formulating learning goals, you can start with your imagined curriculum in which you vividly saw and wrote down what students could do at the end of your course or project. Which of all the things you imagined that your students were doing are the most important, in your opinion? Underline the sentences that reflect the essence of your course or project. Now take these sentences as a starting point for formulating your students' learning goals.

As learning becomes visible and tangible through students' performance, learning goals will try to describe what students are able to do at the end of a lesson, course, or project.[7] To ensure that learning goals reflect the students' performances, you add both content and a verb to those goals. Richard Serra's *Verb List* may offer you some inspiration when it comes to choosing a verb for your learning goal.

Examples of goals that reflect the student's performance:

1. Students <u>can perform</u> *a G-Funk rap based on the catchphrases of their teachers* (Rosa Kijne)
   - <u>can perform</u> = verb
   - *a G-Funk rap based on the catchphrases of their teachers* = content

2. Students <u>can make</u> *a suitcase full of souvenirs from a non-existent holiday*
   - <u>can make</u> = verb
   - *a suitcase full of souvenirs from a non-existent holiday* = content

Main Goals and Subgoals

When designing your curriculum, it can be useful to differentiate between main goals and subgoals (a differentiation teachers may also recognize as 'goals' and 'objectives'). Main goals are broad, overarching goals students ideally will have attained at the end of a complete course or project. For the preceding lessons, teachers can formulate subgoals: smaller goals derived from the main goals that are formulated more specifically and can be achieved in a shorter time frame. By formulating subgoals, teachers can gain insight into whether sufficient time is spent in the lessons on those skills and knowledge that are described in the main goals. Now return to your learning goals, and figure out which goals are overarching main goals, and which ones are subgoals.

Example of a main goal:

Students can compose a one-minute mini-opera about a local news event (Puskas Bartlett, 2019)

Examples of subgoals leading to the attainment of the main goal:

Students can...
• seek out local news events
• discuss which local event is exciting as a topic for a mini-opera
• develop a written or drawn storyline of the mini-opera
• compose the music in a manner that supports the storyline (via recordings, traditional, or any other form of notation)
• stage their opera
• perform their opera live or make a one-minute video of their opera

4.3 Inclusive Learning Goals

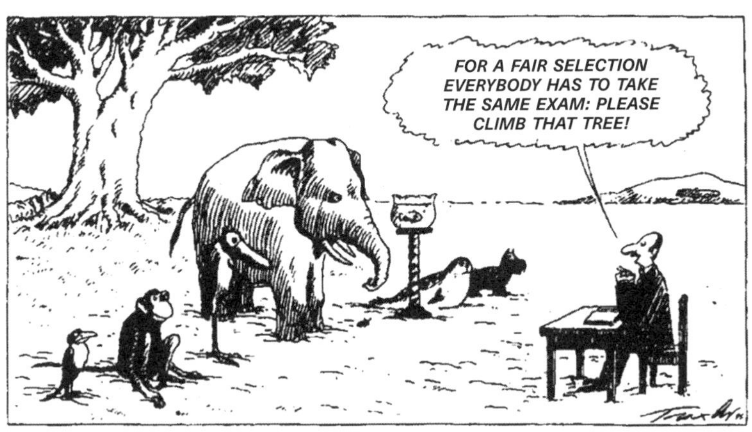

Hans Traxler, *Chancengleichheit* (1983)

As *Wicked Arts Education* aspires to cater to diverse learners,
it can be useful to look at how inclusive your learning goals are.
Main goals that allow for multiple working strategies and multiple
means of expression—as often is the case in arts education—are of
themselves more inclusive than narrowly defined goals. These latter
goals ask for specific working strategies, possibly disadvantaging
certain students who may not be strong in those strategies.[8]

One way to formulate inclusive learning goals is when they are
separated from the means to achieve them.[9] For instance, a learning
goal could be formulated as follows: 'Students can write a story
about their neighbour's dog.' However, if the goal is not per se about
learning to write, but about being able to compose a narrative, this
goal could be reformulated as: 'Students can present a narrative
about their neighbour's dog'. This leaves the possibility open for
students to write, film, act out or draw a narrative, thus opening the
way for a multitude of expressions. Yet, we do believe more closed
learning goals can have a function, too. It can be useful to formulate
more closed goals when teachers want students to learn a specific
skill in a specific arts discipline, or to develop certain knowledge.
Then a more specific goal might be in place.

Inclusivity is also enhanced when you write goals in a language
that is understandable for your students. Lengthy or wordy goals
may look impressive, but are seldom inviting for your students...
or your colleagues.

4.4   Content of Learning Goals

In *Wicked Arts Education*, students' performances will always
be related to the assignments in your curriculum, and the content
of learning goals will, in part, be derived from these assignments.
However, teachers will usually include more learning goals covering
the additional knowledge and skills students will learn during a
lesson, project, or course. For instance, in your backbone curriculum,
you have chosen inspirational sources that may lend themselves
to exemplify a particular theory, and you have noted materials and
techniques you want students to learn. As you start formulating,
do bear in mind that the focus of the content of learning goals can
be different: e.g. you can choose between *arts intrinsic* goals and
cross-curricular goals for your curriculum.

Arts intrinsic goals are goals that refer to learning arts
theory or arts appreciation, developing creative skills within the
arts, or skills and knowledge of arts techniques. As arts educators,
we believe that you should try to strike a balance between these
different artistic goals. Theoretical, creative, or artistic work
might motivate students to explore new materials and techniques,
which allows them to express their ideas. In turn, exposing students
to a variety of materials and techniques can broaden their artistic
knowledge and skills and fuel their creative and conceptual
artistic work.[10]

As arts education may be supportive of developing knowledge
and skills that 'spill over' into other domains, you might also decide
to formulate cross-curricular goals.[11] Well-known cross-curricular
skills are the so-called twenty-first-century skills, which include
critical thinking, problem-solving, collaboration and self-regulation.[12]
Here, too, we believe it is important to strike a balance between arts
intrinsic goals through which students learn the domain of the arts
and cross-curricular (instrumental) ones that may help to develop
skills that are applicable in domains other than the arts.

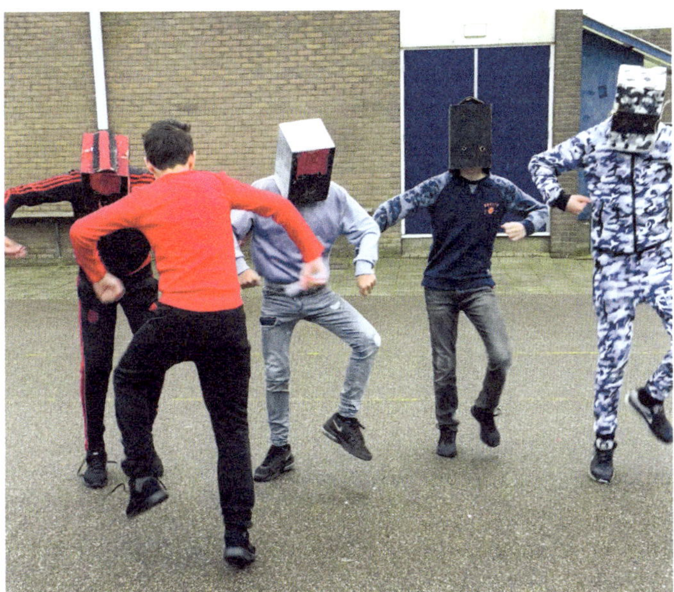

Azaan, Zohab, Ali, Kevin, Nabil, Yassine & Anass, *This is Our Gang*
(2018). Maarten Koole allowed his students to decide on their
learning goals and make what they wanted in his arts lessons.
They took the popular online video game Fortnite as a main source,
and integrated movements and visual elements from the game with
personal views, local influences and actualities in their work

4.5 Playing Around with Goals

Formulating learning goals is not necessarily an easy task and by
no means an exact science.[13] There are no strict guidelines about
how many learning goals teachers should formulate for a course or
project, or precisely how generic or specific they should be. What's
more, teachers can also ask students to formulate their own learning
goals, as this can heighten their intrinsic motivation and their sense
of autonomy.[14, 15] They can add their personal goals to the existing
goals of a course or project or set their own learning goals for the
complete course or project (as illustrated in the image above).

As such, common sense and your experience are useful here:
what is workable in the light of the students, the theme, and
materials you are working with? We simply advise you to formulate
what seems appropriate to your educational context, to experiment
with learning goals and, when needed, to adapt them to make them
more suited to that context. As in the artwork *Polder Cup*: play
around with your goals!

4.6 Design Result: Your Curriculum's Set of Learning Goals

By now, you have more or less decided on the theme, content, and assignment(s) of your curriculum. During this phase, you will have formulated the following for your curriculum:

- Main goals: the curriculum's overarching goals;
- Subgoals: smaller goals derived from the main goals.

Furthermore, you will have checked whether your goals are as inclusive as possible, and whether there is a balance between arts intrinsic and cross-curricular goals.

Next Up: Structuring Your Curriculum

In this chapter you have creatively transformed your imagined curriculum into solid learning goals. The next step is to take the content, assignment, and learning goals of your curriculum and structure them into a coherent curriculum. Guess what? The following chapter will actually provide you with different ways to structure your curriculum meaningfully.

NOTES

1   F. Hoobroeckx and E. M. Haak, *Onderwijskundig ontwerpen* [Educational Design] (Bohn Stafleu van Loghum, 2002).
2   E. Winner, T. Goldstein and S. Vincent-Lancrin, *Art for Art's Sake? The Impact of Arts Education* (OECD, 2013).
3   Hoobroeckx and Haak, *Onderwijskundig ontwerpen*.
4   D. P. Ausubel, *Educational Psychology: A Cognitive View* (Holt, Rinehart and Winston, 1968).
5   T. Seidel, R. Rimmele and M. Prenzel, 'Clarity and Coherence of Lesson Goals as a Scaffold for Student Learning', *Learning and Instruction*, 15(6) (2005), pp. 539–556.
6   Centre for Educational Research and Innovation, *Assessment for Learning Formative Assessment*, paper presented at the OECD/CERI International Conference, 'Learning in the 21st Century: Research, Innovation and Policy', (May 15–16, 2008, Paris).
7   Hoobroeckx and Haak, *Onderwijskundig ontwerpen*.
8   D. Glass, A. Meyer and D. H. Rose, 'Universal Design for Learning and the Arts', *Harvard Educational Review*, 83(1) (2013), pp. 98–119.
9   A. Meyer, D. Rose and D. Gordon, *Universal Design for Learning: Theory and Practice* (CAST Professional Publishing, 2014).
10 C. Hall and P. Thomson, 'Creativity in Teaching: What Can Teachers Learn from Artists?', *Research Papers in Education*, 32(1) (2016), pp. 106–120.
11 E. Winner, T. Goldstein and S. Vincent-Lancrin, 'Art for Art's Sake? The Impact of Arts Education', *Educational Research and Innovation* (OECD Publishing, Paris, 2013).
12 K. Ananiadou and M. Claro, '21st Century Skills and Competences for New Millennium Learners in OECD Countries', *OECD Education Working Papers*, No. 41 (OECD Publishing, 2009).
13 W. Peeters, M. Lucassen, I. Wevers and R. Geurts, *Curriculumontwerp in een notendop*. [Educational Design in a Nutshell] (Vernieuwingsonderwijs, 2021).
14 D. H. Schunk, 'Self-Efficacy for Reading and Writing: Influence of Modeling, Goal Setting and Self-Evaluation', *Reading and Writing Quarterly*, 19 (2003), pp. 159–172.
15 A. Moeller, J. Theiler and C. Wu, 'Goal Setting and Student Achievement: A Longitudinal Study', *Modern Language Journal*, 96(2) (2012), pp. 153–169.

Chapter 5.

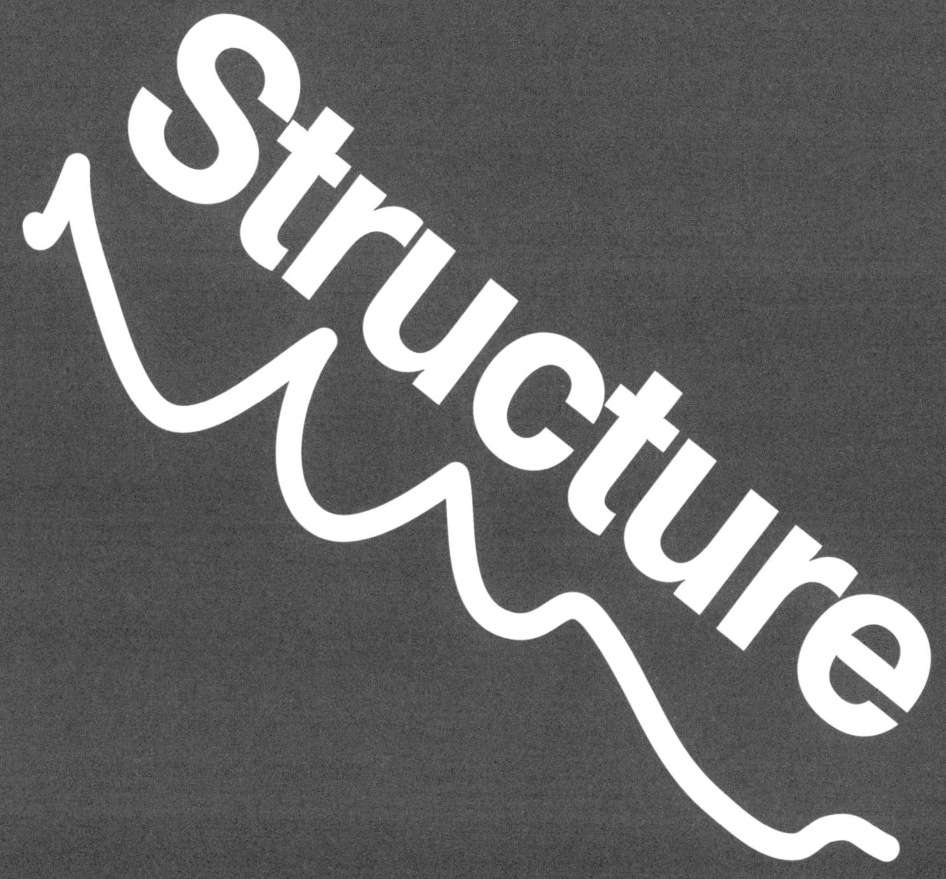

Javanese gamelan is an orchestra of bronze gongs and metallophones, drums, wooden flutes and stringed instruments that together create a rich and distinctive sound. Its music is known for its cyclical nature, in which various types of gongs mark different units within the cycle. For instance, the large gong marks the end of the time cycle, similar to the period in a sentence. Smaller gongs mark smaller units within the cycle, similar to the way that commas and colons mark structures within a sentence. Although the music is clearly structured, Javanese performers have the freedom to drastically vary the tempo and dynamics of a piece, and to improvise on the main melody as they perform it. As such, there is freedom within the given structure, which allows the same piece to always be performed differently.

When we look at curriculum design, we believe that structuring the content of a curriculum is an important design activity. It provides both the teacher and student with a global overview of the whole teaching and learning trajectory, but still allows for a change of pace of teaching and learning or 'on the spot improvising'. The same curriculum on paper, therefore, might look different every time it is performed.

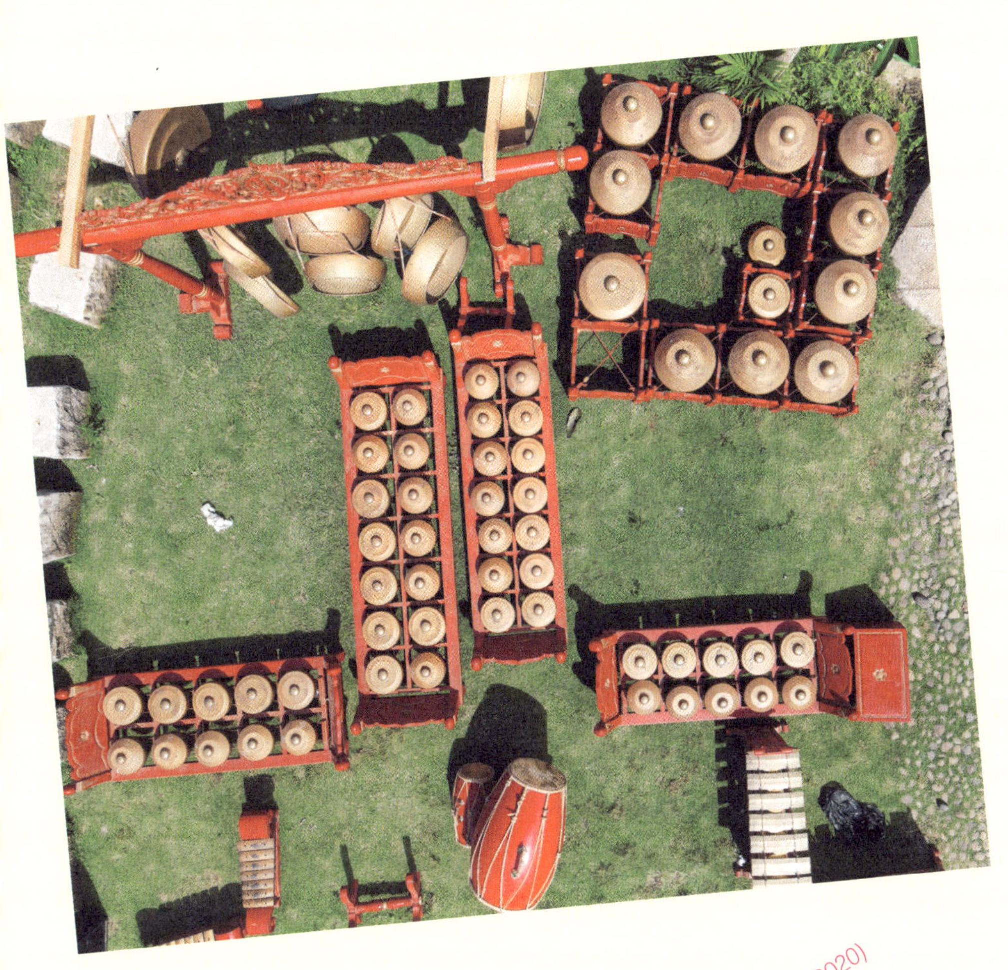

Reezky Pradatatop, Top view of gamelan instruments, Java, Indonesia (2020)

Contents of this chapter

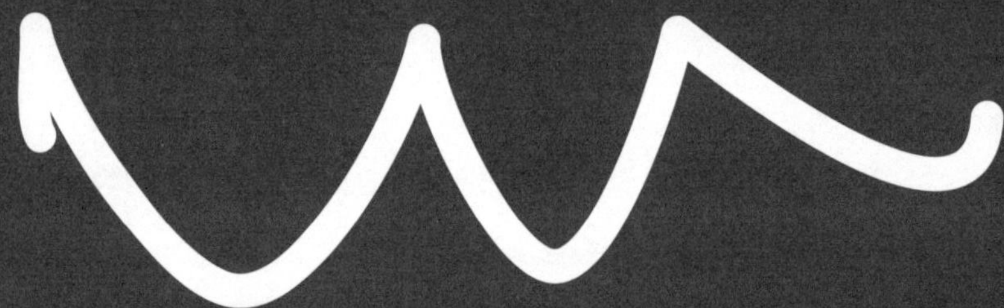

5.1 Structuring the Curriculum

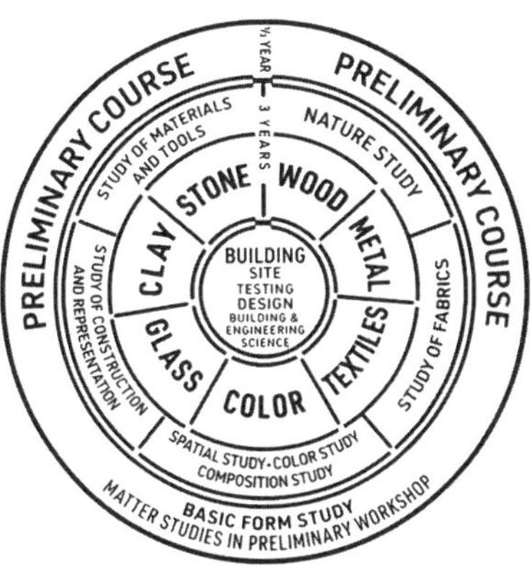

Walter Gropius, Diagram of the Bauhaus curriculum (1922, translated)

In this phase of your design, the challenge of structuring the content, assignment(s), learning goals and activities in an overarching structure lies before you. But before you actually start, it might be good to reflect on *why* structuring a curriculum could be useful. Structuring your curriculum helps you to see when and how students are working on attaining certain learning goals, and whether these goals are realistic within the time and space of a curriculum.[1,2] At the same time, through a structured curriculum students can experience a coherence between parts of the curriculum, and can make connections between lessons more easily. In this phase, you will carefully consider how to divide the learning content, assignments, learning goals, and activities over the available time of a course or project. During that process, you can explore how assignments, skills, and knowledge align, build on each other, connect to or deepen students' prior knowledge and skills.

Curricula can be structured in many ways, and depending on the Wicked Arts Assignment, the learning goals and activities, the educational context, and the timespan of your curriculum, you may choose to structure your curriculum one way or the other. In this chapter, we shall discuss just a few of the possibilities for structuring a curriculum that match with *Wicked Arts Education*. The approaches we show here have in common that they put more emphasis on the content matter of an arts curriculum than a modernist structure based on techniques and materials such as the Bauhaus curriculum.

5.2   Approaches to Structuring Your Curriculum

Realistic Approach

The idea of a realistic approach is that the working processes of (arts) professionals are taken as a starting point to structure the curriculum.[3] A realistic approach fits well with *Wicked Arts Education*, as it enables students to experience how professionals think and work in the domain of the arts. Furthermore, students will often find real-life activities more meaningful as they are relevant to situations beyond school.[4, 5]

Within a realistic approach, generally, a professional activity will not be divided into short activities for students, executed from the easier to the more complex ones under the strict supervision of the teacher. In contrast, students will be exposed to the complexity of a professional activity or an assignment from the start of a lesson or project and guided by the teacher or professional experts. Furthermore, students will be provided with the time, space (e.g., a concert hall), and means (e.g., a budget) to execute the real-life activity. For instance, as a year-long project a class can be tasked to organize an experimental dance performance, from its very first rehearsal to the sales of tickets at a local venue.[6]

In education, different models have been developed for emulating professional (arts) activities. We will discuss two of them that can readily be applied in a *Wicked Arts Education* curriculum.

The Creative Process Model
The cyclical Creative Process Model, developed by the Netherlands Institute for Curriculum Development, is based on the working processes of arts professionals.[7] The model consists of the phases *orientation*, *research*, *execution* and *evaluation*, and throughout every phase *reflection* plays an important role.

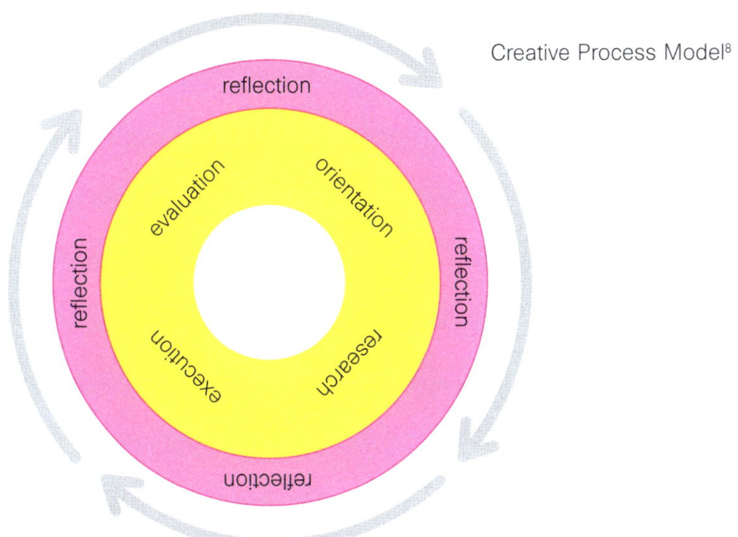

During the *orientation* phase, students explore the presented theme and assignment. Based on various works of art and other inspirational sources, students will discuss the theme and gain ideas for their assignment. Reflection focuses on developing multiple perspectives on the theme. In the next phase, students *research* various possibilities, concepts, or solutions for the assignment. Alone or in a group, they are encouraged to come up with their own concepts and solutions and to make choices about the execution of the assignment, such as the materials they will use. The reflection focuses on the explication of the various choices. After the research phase, students enter the *execution* phase and carry out the assignment. Reflection focuses on the relationship between the choices made in the research phase and the actual execution of the assignment. The *evaluation* phase focuses on the process and product of the assignment, and are discussed in more detail by the teacher and peers. The reflection process is geared towards formulating learning goals that form the start of a subsequent assignment and creative process. Again, the phases of the creative process are not sharply separated but overlap.

Designathon method

The Designathon method is based on how scientists and designers approach problems. This method combines elements of a hackathon, Design Thinking, and Maker-education into a design cycle.[9]

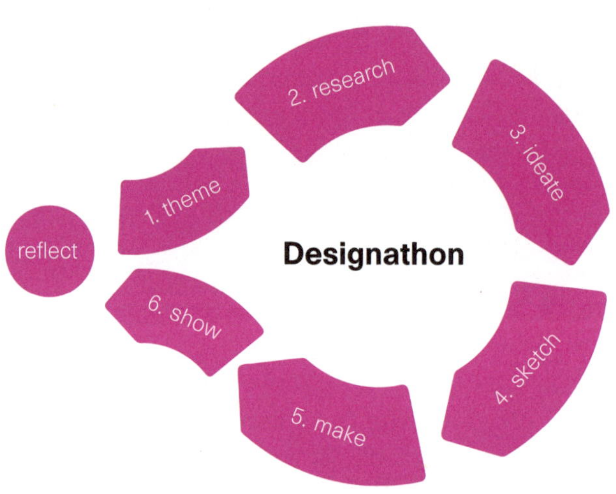

Emer Beamer, Model for the Designathon Method[10]

Usually, a Designathon kicks off with the phase of 'Inspire', in which students are invited to philosophically discuss societal problems around a certain theme, such as waste, food, or water. In the phases 'Research' and 'Ideate' pupils further investigate problems within the offered theme and choose a problem they want to work on. During the 'Sketch' phase, they visualize ideas to solve the problem (design concept), and, in the 'Make' phase, transform a design concept into a prototype. In the phase of 'Show' and 'Reflect' students present their prototypes to each other and reflect on the design process.

The participants of the one-day project Robot Love, for instance, used the Designathon method to structure their project.[11] As a source of inspiration, students first visited the provocative exhibition Robot Love, which explored how persons can accept, or even love, robots (as illustrated in Driessens' and Verstappen's *Tickle Salon 2.0* to the right).

During the phases of 'Research' and 'Ideate', students were introduced to a problem relating to the exhibition: 'How can technology promote tenderness between people?' After investigating and critically discussing this problem, they sketched design concepts and made a prototype of one of their concepts (the 'Sketch' and 'Make' phase). One group of students, for instance, built a robot that functions as an interface between grandchildren and their grandparents: the robot provides grandparents with interesting questions they can ask their grandchildren during a telephone call. During the testing phase, students discussed their prototypes with peers, asking for their critical feedback to improve their prototypes with. The Designathon ended with a presentation of all the prototypes and a reflection on the working process.

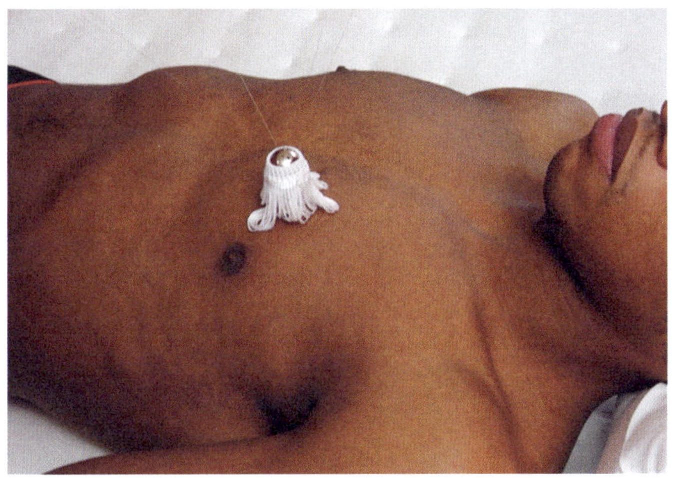

Driessens & Verstappen, *Tickle Salon 2.0* (2018). This artist duo questions with their tickle robots if you would rather be massaged by your loved one or by a small robot? They invite you to experience how perfectly this little brush gets to know your body and your reaction to touch

Game-Based Design Approach

In a game-based design approach game elements and principles are embedded within teaching and learning activities, with the goal to stimulate and sustain students' cognitive and emotional engagement.[12] In this approach, different components of games can be used: from stories, point systems, and badges to classroom response systems. Whatever game elements are chosen, learning emerges from playing the game and ideally promotes problem solving skills.[13]

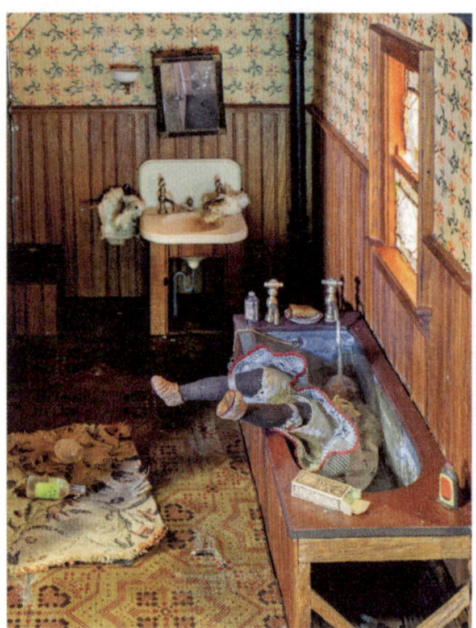

Frances Glessner Lee, Police murder scene scale model (ca 1944)

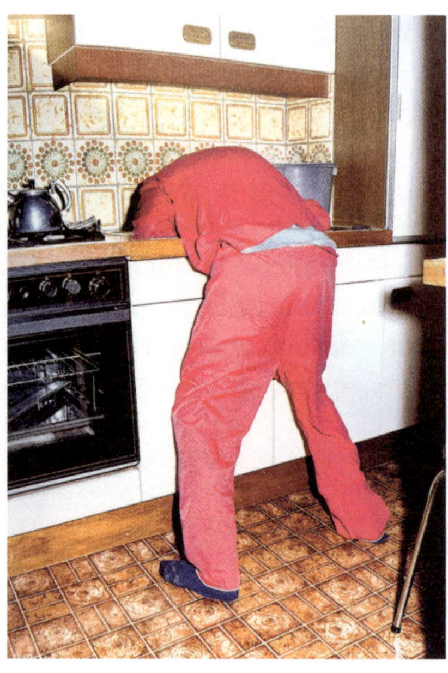

Plaats Delict Amsterdam: Presenting work from the Amsterdam Police Archive (2007)

An example of a game-based curriculum design that relates to *Wicked Arts Education* is the project 'Crime Photography' of art teachers Annemée Dik and Richie Walker. They designed the project for their students in secondary education, using game elements such as a narrative and earning points.[14] In the game, students work for a detective agency that is in danger of going bankrupt. The only way to save the agency from ruin is to fake crime photos that are paid for. Therefore, Dik and Walker task their students with the assignment to 'falsify crime scene photos in groups of three'. The assignment connects to the culture of students as they know crime from books, series, movies, or games, but also to the professional world of photography and societal (ethical) issues of crime.

In the spirit of Glessner Lee (see top-left image) or real police photographers (see top-right image), students stage their own crime photographs. They can earn points, called grants in the game, by taking pictures of certain, unexpected objects, and applying photographic concepts such as perspective and contrast. Students are instructed to accumulate forty points through a maximum of two photographs. As the Dik and Walker project exemplifies, a game-based approach to curriculum design also integrates well with a storyline approach, an approach we will discuss next.[15]

Storyline Approach

Storyline approach uses a narrative to contextualize the teaching and learning of a certain topic.[16] A storyline starts by creating the elements and characters that will bring the narrative to life. Furthermore, each narrative consists of the same structure: a loose 'line' of episodes, with designed key questions per episode. These questions both encourage and support students to further develop the 'story', promoting their engagement and ownership. An important aspect of the storyline approach is that it starts with what students already know, but through questions and activities they further develop their knowledge and skills.[17]

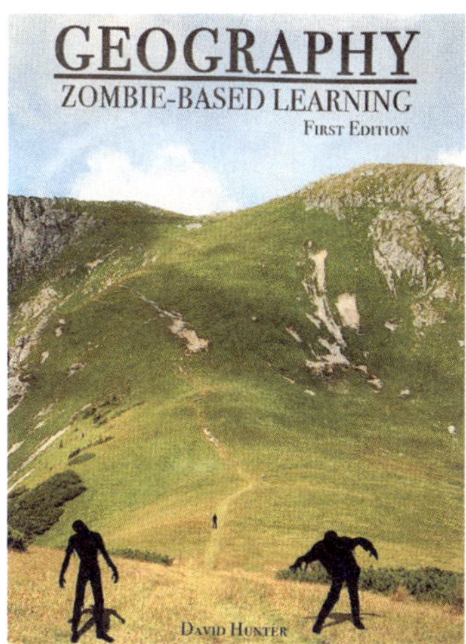

David Hunter, *Zombie-Based Geography* (2018)

Although better-known in primary education, the storyline approach can also be applied in other contexts. For instance, David Hunter based his geography lessons in second education on a topic students are generally thrilled by: the zombie apocalypse story.[18] Through this topic a full middle school geography curriculum is taught, based on the standards for geography that have to be met.

Hunter motivates his students by asking them: 'When the zombies attack, where should you run, where regroup, and where rebuild your life? These questions, key to survival, will help focus your attention on a highly motivating and dangerously overlooked fact: geography skills can save you from the zombie apocalypse!' Hunters' storyline has five different episodes and every episode consists of an assignment:[19]

- planning for the outbreak: news of a zombie-like outbreak is spreading; students have to help to plan just in case an outbreak reaches their community.
- post-outbreak survival: the outbreak has reached your community and chaos follows. Students have to use their skills to try and survive and have to find any other survivors.
- finding a place to settle: you have met with other survivors; students have to try to decide upon a safe place.
- building a new community: decide with your group of survivors to build a safe and sustainable community.
- planning for the future: based on their knowledge of geography and knowledge of the past, students make long-term plans for survival and rebuilding a life.

A storyline approach connects to *Wicked Arts Education* as it employs an artform to design education. When designing your curriculum, you can decide which storyline resonates with the Wicked Arts Assignment. If, for instance, the assignment is 'Design a survival suit for the planet Mars', an expedition to Mars might be an attractive topic for a narrative. Afterwards, you can think of a concrete storyline, divide it into episodes with key questions, and decide on which content matter, learning goals and activities are suitable for which episode.

Thematic Approach

A thematic curriculum organizes teaching and learning experiences such as lessons, courses, or projects around a broad content theme. Within a thematic curriculum, knowledge and skills can continuously be taught and learned within a specific context, providing students with a sense of unity and continuity throughout lessons.[20] Furthermore, this type of curriculum allows teachers to connect a range of different sources about a particular topic, thereby broadening and deepening a theme. Another advantage of a thematic curriculum is that it invites teachers to work interdisciplinarily: knowledge, skills, and working strategies from different (arts) disciplines can be used to explore a certain theme in depth. As such, thematic structuring comes naturally to *Wicked Arts Education,* as it provides students with different inspirational sources that shed light on a theme, aiding them to comprehend it through multiple entry points.

Wicked Arts Education

When designing a thematic curriculum for a longer period, for instance a year, you can reflect on how many themes would be suitable for your students, and how those themes relate to each other: do they build on each other or form a contrast? For instance, Johan de Witt College, an urban high school in The Hague, the Netherlands, developed an interdisciplinary arts curriculum that is structured by themes that have a strong connection with citizenship education. Their second year is divided into four units of nine weeks, consecutively focusing on the themes Sustainability, Power, Diversity and Globalization. During a unit, students work in different disciplines (e.g. dance, theatre, film, music, or the visual arts), but all the assignments have a relationship to the overarching theme.

Another interesting example is how arts history can be thematically structured. Traditionally, Western arts history lessons were structured Eurocentrically and chronologically: students study history units from one point in time to another, such as from the Romanesque Period (1000–1300), to the Gothic Era (1100–1500), to the Renaissance Era (1420–1520), and so forth. In contrast, a thematic approach of an arts history curriculum plans for units, with each unit including content from a range of time periods. In a thematic arts history curriculum, students then might study units such as Feminism and Art, War and Art, Love and Art, Activism and Art, and so forth.

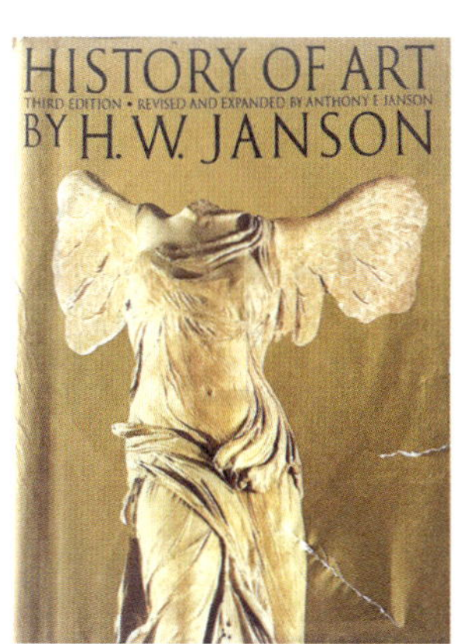

Chronological structuring: Janson's *History of Art* (2015, 8th Edition)

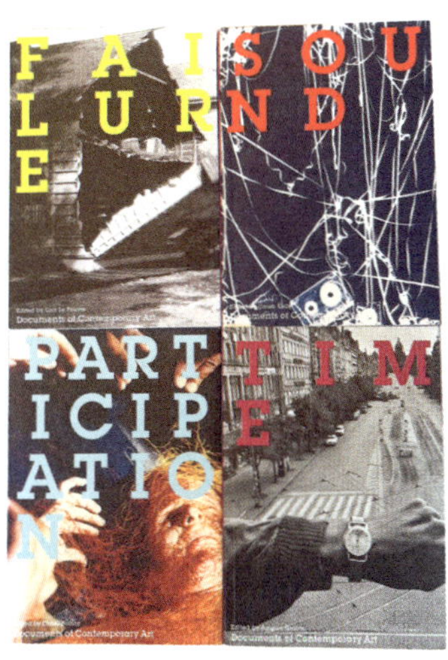

Thematic structuring: Documents of Contemporary Art: *Failure, Sound, Participation, Time* (Whitechapel Gallery/MIT Press (2006 >)

Spiral Curriculum

A spiral curriculum allows students to visit and revisit core themes, concepts, and topics throughout their educational career.[21, 22] The goal of this type of curriculum is for students to consolidate their prior skills and knowledge on certain themes, concepts, and topics, but also to build up both knowledge and skills over time. Thus, a spiral curriculum helps students to gain a deeper and more complex understanding of certain themes, concepts, and topics.

To design a spiral curriculum, you need to start off where your previous project or course ended and decide upon which of the students' prior knowledge and skills you will build on. From there, you will think about which knowledge and skills the students will broaden and deepen, and how you can increase the complexity of learning goals of the new course or project.

In *Wicked Arts Education*, a thematic curriculum and a spiral curriculum can be integrated nicely: a specific theme can be visited in one course or project, which can be revisited and deepened in the next. For instance, during middle school, a music teacher could introduce the theme 'Music for Airports' to its students, centring around the Wicked assignment 'Make music for airports'.[23] In the sixth grade, students could learn about and critically discuss Brian Eno's *Music for Airports* (1978), a landmark album in ambient and electronic music. They could compose ambient 'Airport music' themselves with music software that uses existing loops. In the seventh grade, they can revisit the theme, but then visit an airport, record sounds at the airport, create their own loops based on those sounds, and compose their own Airport music, applying their knowledge on ambient music learned the year before.[24]

week 1	week 2–8	week 9	week 10–16	week 17	week 18–24	week 25	week 26–32	week 33
Premise	*Set Up*	*Turning Point*	*Confron-tation*	*Turning Point*	*Crisis*	*Turning Point*	*Climax*	*The End*
Kick Off	Module 1	Speciali-sation day	Module 2	Speciali-sation day	Module 3	Speciali-sation day	Module 4	Final Presentation

Year-long film curriculum in which four projects and three specialization days have been structured after the phases of a cinematic narrative, Meldrid Ibrahim and Wypke Jannette Walen (2023).

5.3 Choosing a Structure

For your curriculum—a short or long piece of curriculum—you can choose any structuring approach that best suits its content, learning goals and activities. Looking at the realistic approach, a 'realistic' assignment, such as producing an arts festival, can easily span a year's curriculum because students need enough time to execute a plethora of activities to be able to succeed in such a complex task. Yet, if students are tasked with producing a work of art in one or several lessons, the creative process model and the Designathon offer handy realistic approaches to your curriculum. The figure on page 98 shows a realistic ordering at two levels: at the meso level, a year-long film curriculum has been structured according to the phases of a cinema narrative: from 'premise' to 'the end'. In every phase (micro level), students get one film assignment that has been structured after the creative process model. The three 'turning points' are technique-based specialization sessions.

Other structuring approaches also mix and match well, such as the combination of a game-based design approach and a storyline approach. A game-based design can be story-driven, helping students feel more involved and immersed, whereas in a storyline approach, game elements can increase students' engagement. Again, both these approaches can be used in short and long curricula. For instance, you might design a game-based project of three days, or a storyline approach with many episodes that spans a trimester.

Although short curricula with a thematic approach exist, this approach is also great for structuring longer curricula: for example, a year might be divided into four units and each of these units could be allocated a specific theme (see page 96). The fun thing is that you can structure the groups of lessons within these units with a different approach, such as the realistic approaches of the creative process model or the storyline approach. What's more, if you revisit the four themes the following year, you have a spiral curriculum!

So, you can just choose one approach or mix and match different approaches to structure your short or long curriculum. Bear in mind, however, that in the end the structure is there to help students experience a coherence between parts of the curriculum, enhancing their engagement and learning process.

5.4 Putting Structuring into Practice

Once you have decided on the structure of your curriculum, start dividing the content and subgoals over its different phases. For instance, if you decide on the Creative Process Model for your curriculum, you can first write down each phase, and then roughly divide the content and subgoals over each of those phases. Lastly, decide on the time needed for these different phases. Depending on the complexity of the theme or the assignment and the students you will be teaching, you might need more or less time for the different phases.

Phases Creative Process Model	Subgoals needed to attain the main goals	Time
Orientation phase explore the theme and assignment of the project	content + subgoals	one lesson
Research phase research various concepts or solutions for the assignment	content + subgoals	two lessons
Execution phase carry out the assignment	content + subgoals	three lessons
Evaluation phase present and evaluate the (working) process and product of the assignment	content + subgoals	one lesson

Structured curriculum based on the Creative Process Model

5.5 Design Result: Your Curriculum's Structure

You are really on a roll now with your curriculum! By now you have:

- chosen the structure of your curriculum;
- divided the content and subgoals over the different phases of that structure;
- decided on how much time you approximately need for each phase.

Now is probably also a good time to start looking back as well. Through the process of structuring, you might find that you have too many or not enough learning goals, or that some goals are lacking. If you, therefore, decide to alter your learning goals, you may want to look back even further at your curriculum to see if anything needs changing there, too.

Next Up: Choosing and Designing Learning Activities for Your Curriculum

The next step in your curriculum design is to further flesh it out with learning activities. In the following chapter you will be enticed to transform your learning goals and content into exciting and varied learning activities for your curriculum.

NOTES

1   F. Hoobroeckx and E. M. Haak, *Onderwijskundig ontwerpen* [Educational Design] (Bohn Stafleu van Loghum, 2002).

2   W. Peeters, M. Lucassen, I. Wevers and R. Geurts, *Curriculumontwerp in een notendop* [Curriculum Design in a Nutshell] (Uitgeverij OMJS, 2022).

3   Hoobroeckx and Haak, *Onderwijskundig ontwerpen*.

4   D. Glass, A. Meyer and D. H. Rose, 'Universal Design for Learning and the Arts', *Harvard Educational Review*, 83(1) (2013), pp. 98–119.

5   E. Roelofs and J. Terwel, 'Constructivism and Authentic Pedagogy: State of the Art and Recent Developments in the Dutch National Curriculum in Secondary Education', *Journal of Curriculum Studies*, 31(2) (1999), 201–227.

6   Glass, Meyer and Rose, *Universal Design for Learning and the Arts*.

7   Netherlands Institute for Curriculum Development, *Het creatieve proces* [The Creative Process] (2019), www.slo.nl/thema/vakspecifieke-thema/kunst-cultuur/leerplankader-kunstzinnige-orientatie/leerlijnen/informatie/creatieve-proces/.

8   Ibid.

9   E. Beamer Cronin and D. H. Hyman, 'Where MakerEd meets Change-Maker ED: The journey to the classroom', P. Troxler and R. Klapwijk (eds.), *Proceedings of FabLearn Netherlands 2018* (Eindhoven: Fablearn Netherlands, 2018), pp. 34–42.

10   E. Beamer, 'Designathon', *Praxisbulletin*, 34(7) (2017), pp. 84–87.

11   M. Bremmer, E. Heijnen, A. Hotze, M. Pijls, E Beamer and N. Roos, 'ArtsSciences Design-a-thon: Solving Complex Problems in Interdisciplinary Teams', *European Journal of STEM Education*, 6(1) (2021), pp. 2–10.

12   L. Sheldon, *The Multiplayer Classroom: Designing Coursework as a Game* (Cengage, 2011).

13   Ibid.

14   A. Dik. and R. Walker, *Misdaadfotografie in de kunstles* [Crime Photography in the Art Class], Kunstzone.

15   Ibid.

16   P. Tarrant, *A Practical Guide to Using Storyline Across the Curriculum: Inspiring Learning with Passion* (Routledge, 2019).

17   Ibid.

18   D. Hunter, *Zombie-Based Geography: Outbreak* (Interact, 2018).

19   Ibid.

20   G. Ward, 'Using Theme Cycles', M. B. Sampson, T. V. Rasinski, M. R. Sampson (eds.), *Total Literacy: Pathways to Reading, Writing and Learning* (Wadsworth Pub Co, 2003).

21   J. S. Bruner, *The Process of Education* (Vintage, 1960).

22   Hoobroeckx and Haak, *Onderwijskundig ontwerpen*.

23   B. Appermont, E. Schrooten and F. Verneert, *Tijd voor Maken 2, creëren met groepen.* [Time to Create 2, Creating with Groups] (Hal Leonard, 2022).

24   Ibid.

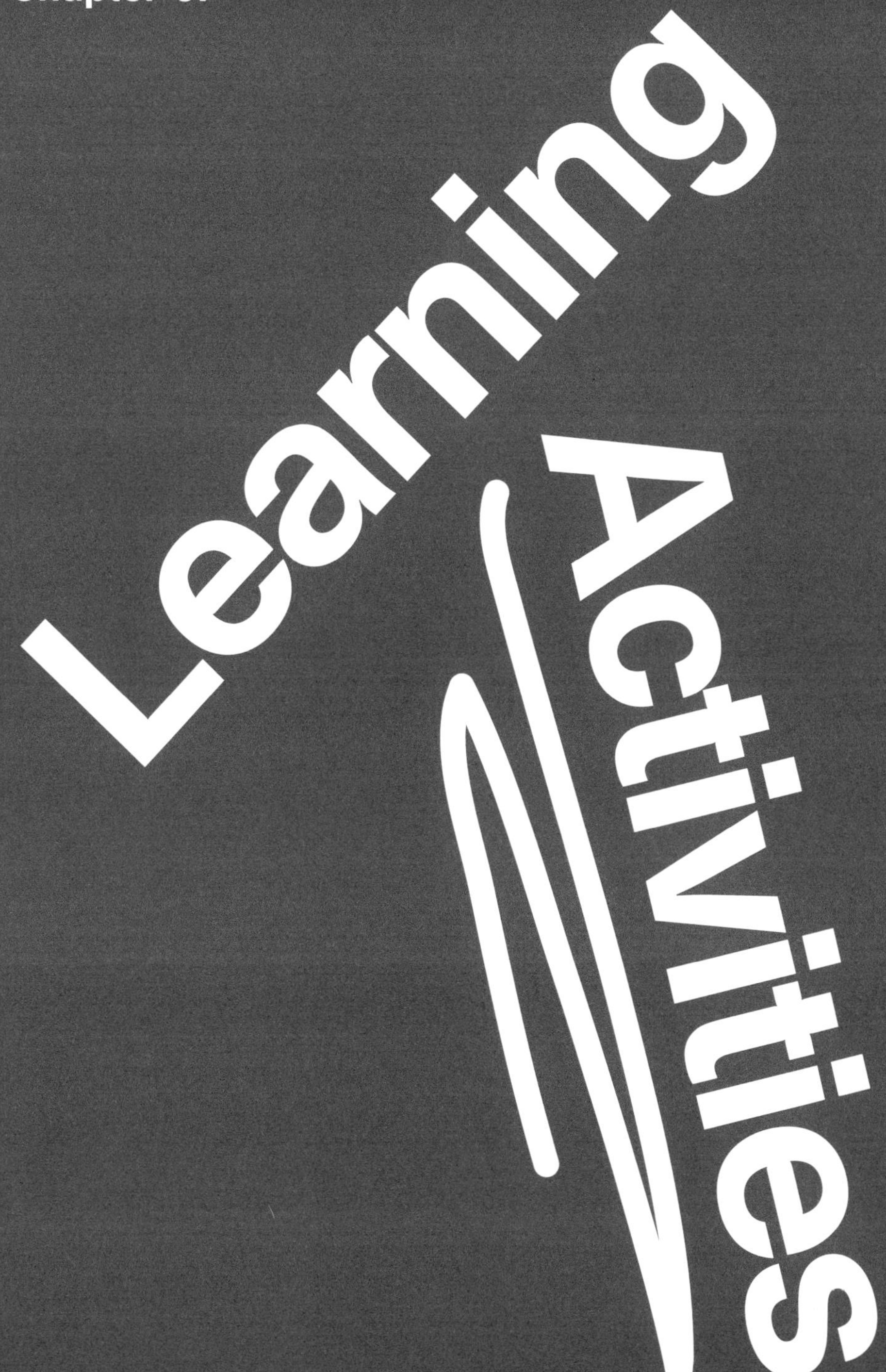
Learning Activities

Although Dutch artist Anouk Kruithof is not a dance teacher, her video installation *Universal Tongue* feels like an infectious display of informal learning activities in dance. Together with an international team, Kruithof collected 8800 videos with fragments of people dancing solo, in pairs or in groups, found on YouTube, Instagram and Facebook. 250 hours of video material that were reduced to 1,000 dance styles from 196 countries from all over the world. On huge screens, styles such as Kuduru, vogue, Klezmer, Fortnite, twerking, or Sufi alternate at a rapid pace, accompanied by an eclectic soundtrack. In an accompanying publication, the origin, background and meaning of every one of 1000 dance styles are described in alphabetical order, from Abakuá-Dance (Cuba) to Zydeco (USA).

From an educational perspective, *Universal Tongue* can be seen as a celebration of collective dance expertise in the era of the Internet. Each of the dance styles has distinctive moves and sequences, often learned through endless training and practice. One of the most creative challenges for educational designers is to transform learning objectives into learning activities that are as vibrant and engaging as seen in *Universal Tongue*. In a Wicked Arts Curriculum, learning activities breathe life into a learning programme by describing in detail what students and their teachers do.

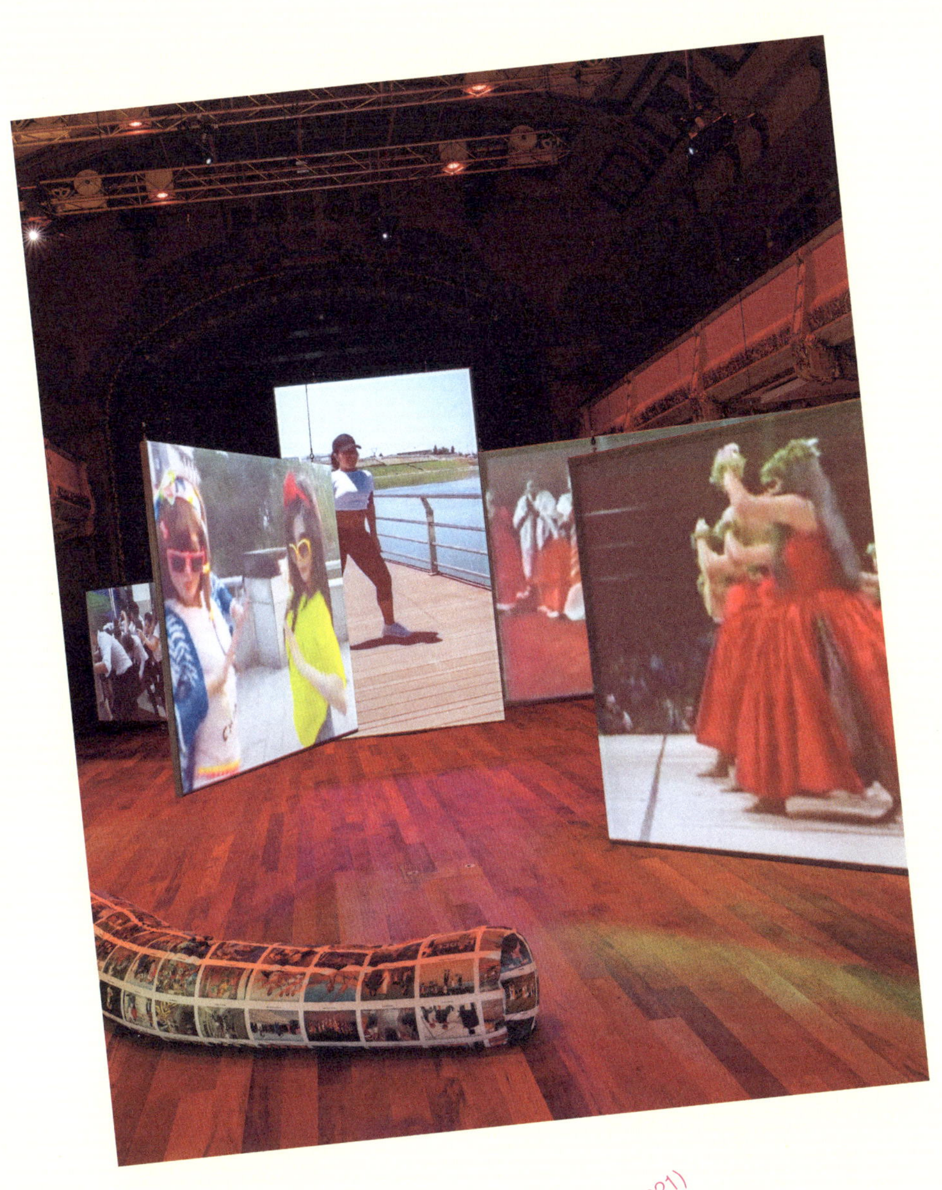

Anouk Kruithof, *Universal Tongue* (2021)

Contents of this chapter

6.1   Using Learning Activities

When you imagine a curriculum as a building, learning activities are the 'bricks'. Learning activities describe what students and their teachers do in detail, thus demonstrating how learning goals are operationalized.[1] Every teacher uses learning activities, for instance, giving verbal instructions, working in groups or giving students individual feedback, but not everyone makes them explicit in their educational design. By treating learning activities as building blocks in your educational design, your teaching methods become more explicit, offering you possibilities to rethink and update your teaching habits. Furthermore, such explicit learning activities stimulate teacher-collaboration, as they make your educational design more transparent and transferable.

Active Learning

Describing your learning activities also helps you to check who is doing the hard work in class, the student or … the teacher? Who does not recognize the image of the teacher who is intensely discussing the fine details of some neo-Expressionist work, while most of the class is looking dreamily at the passing cars outside? Research has shown that students learn deeper when they actively construct meaning by mentally reorganizing information and integrating it with the knowledge they already possess.[2,3] This notion is called active or generative learning and fits in with the social-constructivist premise of *Wicked Arts Education* that new knowledge sticks with us better when we have summarized, analysed, discussed, re-ordered or applied it in new situations. Describing student and teacher activities during the different phases of a course reveals whether students are challenged to learn actively. For instance, should you notice that during one hour the student activity is 'listening', a more active learning activity is called for.

Varied Learning

Some teachers may state that a three-hour arts class is too much for the students' attention span, or that a traditional school timetable with another subject every forty-five minutes provides variety in learning. Neither of these statements is really true: a well-balanced mix of learning activities can make a lesson of three hours accessible, and every forty-five minutes a different teacher who is plenary lecturing can still feel pretty monotonous. Variety is the spice of learning and keeps students more engaged. This also applies to the productive parts of your lesson or project. Learning activities such as student-presentations of concepts, skits and sketches, and intermediate critiques in small groups, can provide more variation and focus during creative processes.[4] Moreover, offering varied learning activities to study the same subject matter can improve the learning process.[5] Variation challenges you to rethink an underlying problem from different angles, preventing students from endlessly applying the same learning strategy. As such, variety in learning activities makes your lessons more diverse and helps your students to learn more deeply.[6]

6.2 Types of Learning Activities

As *Universal Tongue* exemplifies, there are thousands of learning activities, which vary from those that are well-established and used all over the world to that original exercise thought up by a single arts teacher. Rather than making an endless list of learning activities, we will discuss and give some examples of learning activities that are in line with *Wicked Arts Education*, grouped under: *introduction and orientation, theory and arts appreciation, research and arts production*, and *presentation and assessment*. The learning activities discussed below are not arranged in strictly chronological order. For example, theory and arts appreciation may be strategically scheduled before, after, or during arts production.

Introduction and Orientation

Based on her research in 2019, Nathalie Roos introduced a project about arts, protest, and activism by giving students the counter-intuitive assignment to 'do the opposite of different teacher inst-ructions for five minutes'. Through this learning activity, she playfully engaged students and introduced them actively to the topic of the course.

As the introduction is the first moment that your students are involved in a new curriculum, establishing meaningful connections between the culture of the student and the upcoming programme is a central concern. Many arts projects start off with playful game-like exercises including dance freeze-games, body percussion, or theatrical word/movement improvisations. Although such intro-ductions can work great as social icebreakers and energizers, when there is no orientation towards the learning goals of the course, they may feel random or empty. So, try to make these activities more meaningful by connecting them to the learning goals and by using them to activate the student's prior knowledge in connection with the content and skills of the upcoming course.[7]

Also, a work of art or popular culture may give students a good entry point into your curriculum. Check the sources you selected in your backbone curriculum and see which source or REO has the capacity to introduce the upcoming programme in a stimulating way. When such an introduction takes place in a real-life setting, or when the artist is actually present, your introduction will probably gain even more relevance or urgency!

Theory and Arts Appreciation

As we encounter the arts as an interplay between body and mind, studying arts-related histories, stories or concepts and discussing works of popular culture and the arts are vital aspects of Wicked Arts Curricula, in addition to producing art. Remarkably, during class observations, we often note that arts teachers may fall back on tradi-tional instruction forms during (arts) theory and arts appreciation lessons.[8] Increasing your 'teacher-toolbox' with more diverse and active learning activities for teaching theory and arts appreciation will make your courses more interactive and effective. Moreover, they assist students with diverse abilities in exploring the arts in diverse ways and using varied learning strategies effectively.

Active Learning Activities for Theory

Fiorella and Mayer have listed general evidence-based learning strategies that support students to construct meaning actively, connecting new ideas with their existing knowledge.[9] Many of these strategies can also be applied in arts education. For instance, *summarizing and mapping* information helps students to synthesize and re-order new information. Students could be asked to briefly jot down or present what the cinematic style 'film noir' entails, or they could make a mind map of the different aspects of the hip hop movement.

Learning strategies that involve *drawing* or *enacting* theoretical material have also proven to be fruitful. These strategies stimulate embodied forms of learning, which we are so familiar with in the arts. Asking students to sketch a typical Gothic church or to clap a 7/8th measure provides support to understanding complex, language-based concepts.

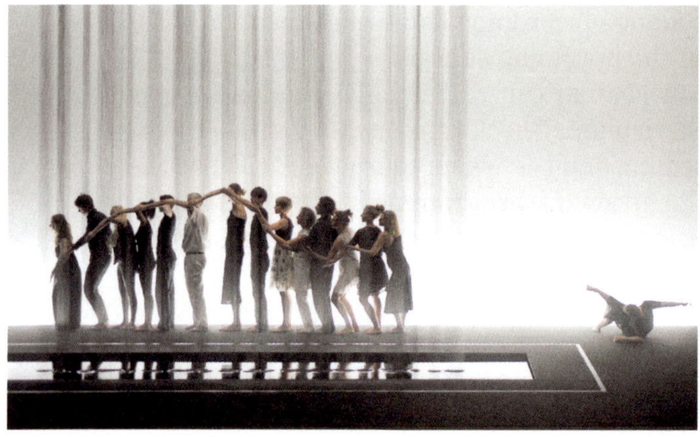

Gabriela Lang, *Performative guided tour through ZKM (Centre for Art and Media)* (2023). Rather than focusing on verbal information transfer, this embodied museum tour is based on enactment as a learning strategy

Lastly, *self-explaining* and *teaching* by students are also effective learning strategies for the understanding of theoretical concepts. In arts lessons, students could be asked to think out loud, while analysing a work in a museum or to explain to a peer what the difference is between a story's protagonist and antagonist.

In the table on the next page, we listed a few active learning activities that can be implemented quite easily.

Think-share-exchange

Rather than asking the class 'are there questions?', or addressing only one student, this simple learning activity makes the whole group active. *Think-share-exchange* is especially suitable for open questions that allow different or complimentary answers.
- The teacher asks a question to all students;
- Students are given time to think in silence about that question (you can also ask them to write down their answers);
- Then the students discuss their answers in pairs;
- Lastly, the teacher randomly asks some students for their answer.

Rapid duo check

This learning activity can be used to check questions or tasks that only have one correct answer, like years, names, styles, characteristics or multiple choice questions.
- Students first do a task or homework individually;
- Once the work is finished, each student compares their own results or answers to those of a fellow student. Because only one correct response is possible, students must reach a consensus;
- Possible extra step: two duos compare and check their answers;
- Lastly: the teacher only discusses the answers that the duos could not agree upon, as all the other answers may be considered 'unproblematic'.

Expert groups

This activity is especially suitable when students have to study a bigger theme that can be divided into different sub-themes.
- Students are divided into groups;
- Each group member is assigned to content matter that has been divided into equivalent and logical parts;
- Each student individually studies one part of the material;
- Optional step: students who study the same part of the material may sit together for consultation;
- Then each student presents the studied material to the other members of the original group;
- Now all group members should be familiar with all the subject matter.

Three learning activities for regular use, that challenge students to study theory in an active manner

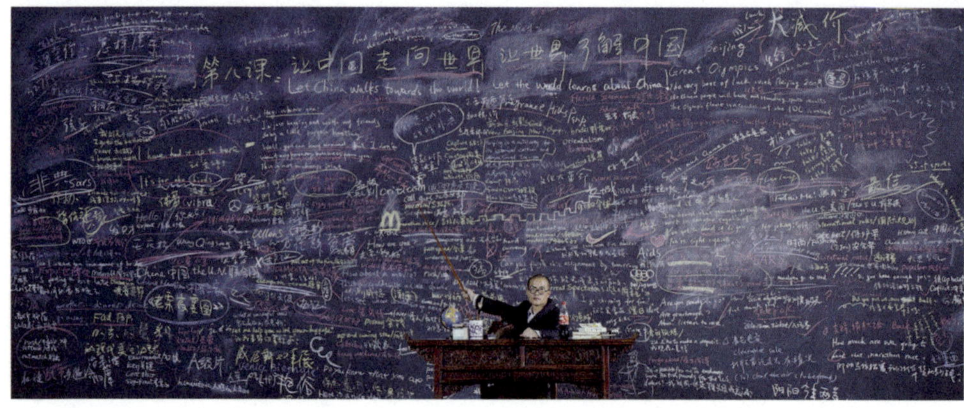

Wang Qingsong, *Follow Me* (2003)

Multimedia Learning

Students learn and remember new information better when it is presented both verbally and visually.[10, 11] As you are teaching about popular culture and the arts, video, audio and still images can all be used for arts appreciation and to explain or illustrate various ideas or concepts in an accessible way. But, as Wang Qingsong shows in *Follow Me*, bombarding your students with an overwhelming amount of texts and images is not really an effective form of multimedia learning. Based on his ongoing research, Mayer[12] formulated some really useful design principles that can be applied in presentations and other teaching materials for arts education. In the table below we have listed a few of these multimedia design principles.

The pre-training principle. Defining key terms and concepts in advance helps students learn more deeply from a multimedia message. Before you start your passionate lecture about contemporary sustainable architecture, give your students a handout with the key terms for the presentation (e.g. names, definitions, characteristics).

The coherence principle. Students learn better when irrelevant material is excluded. As an arts teacher, you might be tempted to creatively spice up your handouts and slides abundantly. Sparingly use decorations, background images/music and other cool but unrelated materials.

The modality principle. Students learn more deeply from pictures with spoken words than from pictures with printed words. Avoid using too much on-screen text in your presentations, unless they list key elements, provide references or when texts function as subtitles for deaf or foreign students.

All 12 design principles for multimedia learning can be found online.[13]

Design principles for multimedia learning

Learning Activities for Exchanging Ideas and Opinions
Because what we see and experience as 'artistic' is intersubjective and dynamic, discussion and meaning making is inherent to the arts and an important aspect of *Wicked Arts Education*. A way to empower students individually to discuss issues related to their culture, the arts, or society is to ask them to first write down ideas and opinions, then collect them and discuss the results plenary. Also, exchanging ideas and opinions in smaller groups can intensify students' focus and provide a safer discussion space. The use of renowned debate formats can similarly provide useful formats for group conversations, such as a *roleplay debate* in which students form teams with assigned stakeholders who defend a certain viewpoint.[14]

As for appreciation of specifically the arts, we recommend drawing on existing approaches that can help you to design and guide arts analysis and criticism sessions, both in and out of school, such as *Criticizing Art,*[15] *Visual Thinking Strategies,*[16] *Critical Thinking in Music,*[17] or *Art-Based Learning.*[18] Rather than asking students to use formalistic analysis lists, these approaches emphasize critical thinking and meaning making through arts appreciation via open questions, such as: 'What's going on in this music?' 'What do you hear that makes you say that?' and 'What more can I find?'[19] You will find that meaning-making processes in the arts are often varied, depending on the background knowledge and experience of students, as well as the contextual information that has been provided to them.[20] See table on the next page.

Artist-teacher Oskar Maarleveld developed *Wicked Ways of Watching (WWOW): Unconventional learning activities for analysis and reflection in exhibitions*. Some examples:

Art lover / art hater

Students form duos and pick an artwork in an exhibition. By chance, they get assigned a role as either someone who loves the artwork, or as someone who is very critical of the work. From their perspective, they discuss and endeavour to persuade each other with arguments. Through this role play, students learn to analyse and discuss the arts from perspectives that may differ from their own.

Artwork as a gift

Students choose an artwork in an exhibition as a gift for a fellow student. Once the work is chosen, they explain it to either the student or to the entire group. In this learning activity, art appreciation is tied to engaging with a peer's personality and interests.

Turning your back to art

A student or group is positioned with their back to the artwork, while another student describes it precisely. The description has to be done so lively that the other student(s) can retell or draw the work themselves. Here students learn to analyse, describe, or imagine artworks meticulously.

Staging art

In groups, students make a tableau vivant of a work they choose in an exhibition. One student is the director/photographer, another takes care of the visual aids and props. As such, students learn to actively explore the composition of an artwork and the expression and posture of the characters depicted.

Wicked Ways of Watching

Research and Arts Production

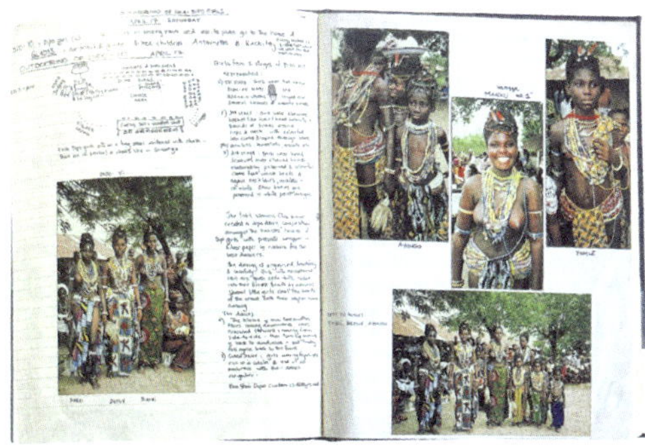

Excerpt from:
Jennifer New,
Drawing from Life
(2005)

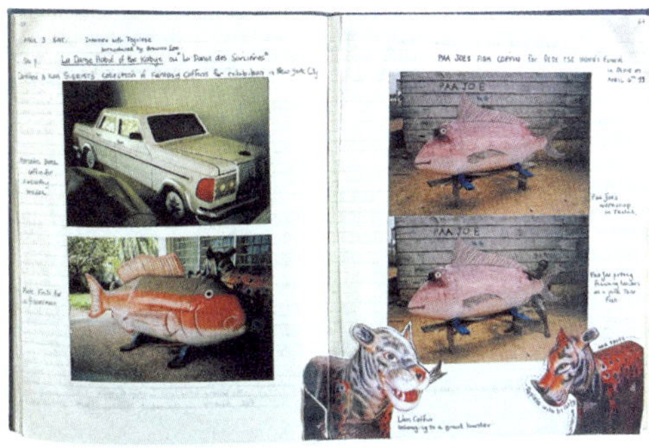

Wicked Arts Education often includes research phases in which various sources are studied, ideas are developed and tried through experiments, improvisation, or sketches. Below we discuss some learning activities that can offer your students support during that precarious phase of research, idea development, and experimentation.

Webquests and other forms in which students collect information within a given timeframe, can motivate students to quickly research and select information individually or in small groups. Where webquests help you to collect useful online resources, making *harvest maps*[21] helps students to identify the available materials and human resources in the offline world. Harvest mapping usually starts by drawing a circle on a map around the educational institution with a diameter of, say, 500 metres, as seen on the next page. Then students are asked to map out all the material and human resources within that circle that could be useful for a (social) arts project. Using this approach, students of the Amsterdam Breitner Academy designed fashion accessories made from cat hair to support an animal shelter. Another group made in situ soundscapes, based on the stories and objects they collected in a local vintage shop.

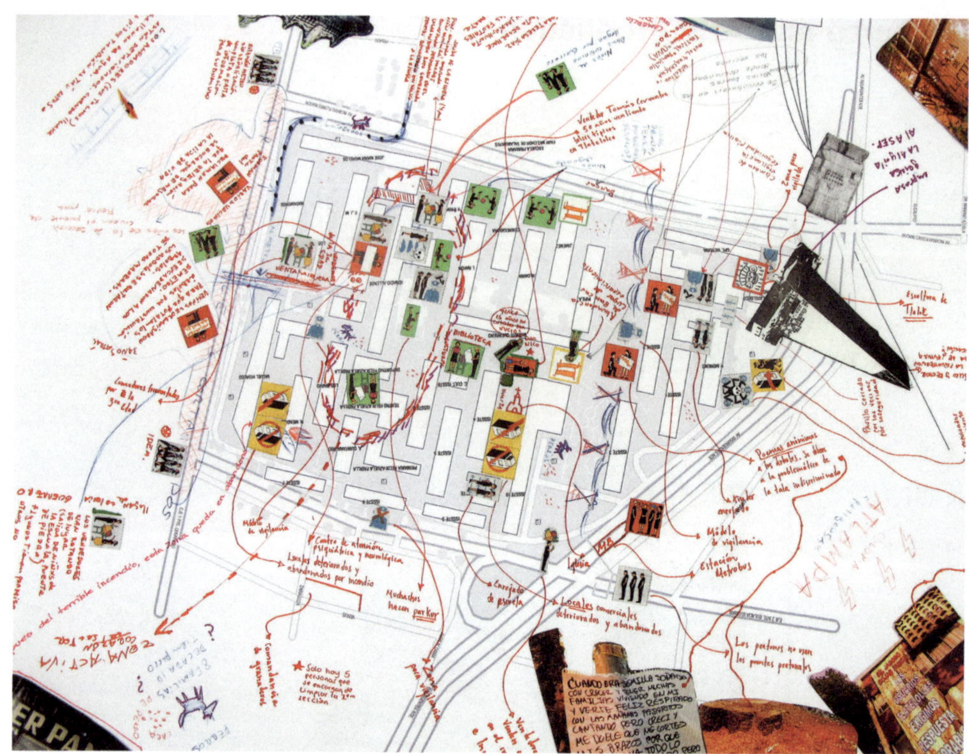

Julia Risler and Pablo Ares, *Harvest Map of a Neighbourhood of Mexico City, Mexico* (2012)

For idea development, *brainstorms* in written or other forms can help students to assemble ideas rapidly. Keep in mind that when making lists, individual brainstorms are usually more productive. When students have to find solutions for a complex task, group brainstorms might produce better results.[22] Jennifer New sees *journals* as 'the unsung heroes,[23] the working stiffs of creative life' (see page 115). Keeping a journal or *portfolio* (see chapter 7) can help individual students to collect ideas, sources of inspiration, and sketches at any moment of the day. Digital journals such as Padlet Wall offer extra possibilities, such as adding moving images and sound and different forms of collective journaling.

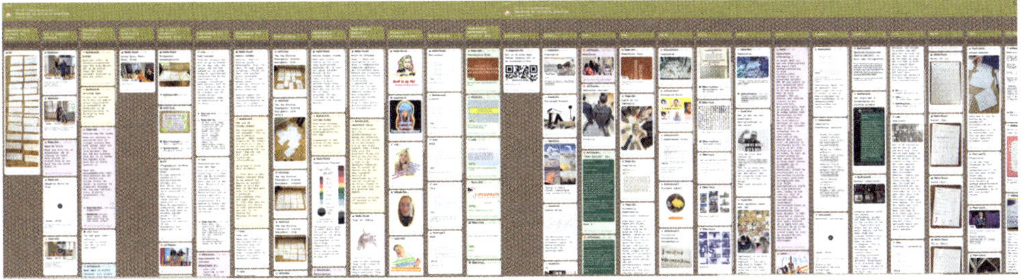

Digital online group journal using Padlet Wall (2023)

Even when your students are totally absorbed in arts experimentation and production, they can benefit from using varied learning activities. *Intermediate presentations* and *try-outs* help students to show and discuss what they are making, what they have done, and how they want to proceed. *Intermediate feedback* (see chapter 7) can also be a great help in making improvements during the making process. Think about variations on the common strategies of 'teacher models' or 'teacher goes around class': students can give each other peer feedback in smaller or larger groups, or you may organize small group critic sessions in which both the teacher and some students participate. You can even invite artists or other experts to participate in group or individual feedback sessions.

Presentation and Assessment

Although presentations and assessments usually end a course or project, they are also crucial during the learning process as they provide students with formative feedback that they can use to improve their work (see chapter 7). Therefore, presentations and assessments deserve a detailed design as learning activities too. As a teacher, you can take some issues into account when designing learning activities for presentation, assessment, and reflection sessions.

As *Wicked Arts Education* strives for authentic learning experiences, you could consider moving presentations into real-life settings, either on- or offline. For instance, a dance teacher regularly posts her students' short choreographies on TikTok, and a group of music teachers present their student bands in a local music venue. Do keep in mind that real-life settings bring real-life challenges with regard to organization, finances and mutual expectations. And even when you decide to present learning results in an educational institution, a small spatial intervention into a school's setting (e.g. rearranging furniture, changing the light) can still contribute to the 'realness' of the student's presentation.

There is of course much more at stake when others than the students themselves visit presentations. Having external visitors can make a presentation lively and meaningful. However, the social safety of your students has to be taken into account. When students are inexperienced or insecure about their results, an intimate setting without any external guests could be the better choice.

Furthermore, do not miss out on opportunities to engage your students during presentations and assessment processes. Self-explaining and teaching are effective learning strategies for students, as we have discussed.[24] Students could prepare written or spoken 'artist statements' that accompany their presentation, while their peers and teachers act as engaged audiences.

As part of the assessment process, students can be invited to critically reflect on their learning process, product, theory, or on the collaboration with peers.[25] Nowadays students can document their reflections on what went well or what could be improved in different ways: they can write, use visuals, audio, or video.

There are, however, some points of concern when it comes to reflecting as a group or individually. For instance, plenary reflections with the whole class may seem an attractive way of reflecting but can result in only the most enthusiastic or well-spoken students participating. When students reflect simultaneously in small groups (e.g. from two to five students), the threshold to take part is lower and each student gets more time to reflect and share. Another concern is that reflection can turn into a fill-in-the-blank exercise, with students filling in a reflection checklist like zombies.[26] So, beware of an overkill of reflection: vary the ways of reflecting and use reflection meaningfully for your students. Lastly, reflection and feedback are intimately related; in chapter 7 we will take a closer look at different forms of feedback and at self- and peer-assessment. In the following table we have listed a few examples of accessible reflection activities.

Reflection on the process: Video reflection

The student places a video fragment of two minutes of their choreography, composition, scene or any other work of art in progress on an online platform or digital portfolio and writes down a relevant topic or question they want their peers to reflect on. At least two peers reflect on the video fragment and provide comments.

Reflection on the product: The gossip method

A group reflects on an artwork and, as if they are gossiping, they talk about the maker in the third person ('The maker has…'). The maker pretends they are not there, steps out of the circle and listens in. This method usually elicits more honest reflections and can therefore only be applied if the group is a safe environment. Based on DAS Theatre.[27]

Reflection on the theory: One-minute reflection[28]

Students are instructed to write down the essence of a theory they learned about in no more than one minute. They are asked: 'What were the most important concepts discussed in this theory?' Students read out or hand in their answers. The teachers can check if the main theoretical concepts are recognized and understood.

Reflection on the collaboration: De Bono roleplay

During a group project, group members are asked to reflect on the process so far. While reflecting, each group member takes on a given role, based on one of the six 'thinking hats' as identified by De Bono.[29] By mentally wearing one of the six hats, each student reflects on the collaborative process from another perspective: The white hat calls for facts and information; the red hat expresses feelings and emotions; the green hat comes with new ideas, the black hat focuses on threats and weaknesses, the yellow hat focuses on strengths and opportunities; and the blue hat manages the reflection process.

Reflection activities

T
I
P

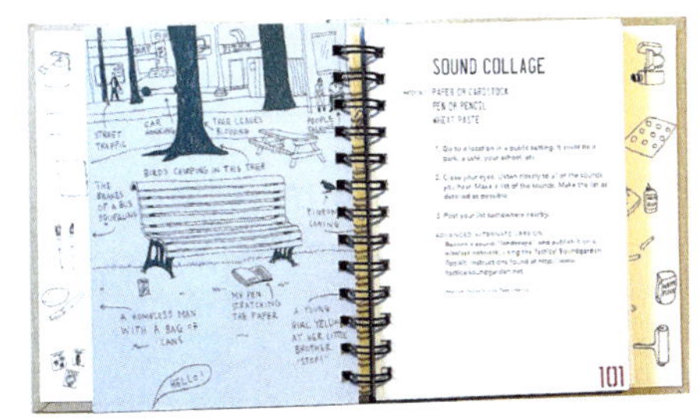

Keri Smith, *The Guerilla Art Kit* (2007)

Worksheets and other instructional materials can offer students creative forms of support during all phases of an arts course or project.

6.3 Guiding *Wicked Arts Education*

Active and varied learning activities do not imply that students should be left to their own devices.[30, 31] Teachers still play a crucial role in guiding their students during their learning process.

Guiding Active Learning Activities

Keep in mind that the use of active learning activities and open, Wicked assignments can be challenging for students because they have to be more active, think deeper, make more mistakes and interact more with others than in traditional lessons.[32] Students may even resist some learning activities because they rely on earlier developed learning strategies that feel more comfortable, but are actually less effective (e.g.: cramming arts theory, choosing a first idea during a creative process, postponing creative work until the final deadline),[33] It is therefore desirable to openly discuss learning strategies with your students, and use scaffolding to get students acquainted with (inter)active learning and Wicked Arts Assignments.

Guiding Collaboration

As *Wicked Arts Education* advocates that students and their teachers operate as learning communities, collaboration is an important feature (which does not mean that individual assignments are taboo). However, simply giving group assignments will not result automatically in fruitful student collaboration. In groups, students can experience logistical problems (high workload, scheduling the work), social problems (poor communication, conflicts), leading to a decrease in motivation.[34] Successful group work needs the right circumstances, attention to group skill development and perhaps above all, a teacher who actively and critically guides the process.

Johnson and colleagues[35] formulated five essential components of cooperative learning that can be used as a checklist for guiding group processes. We have added some concrete guidelines that help to meet these criteria.

- *Positive interdependence*: Group members perceive that they 'sing in harmony or drift in dissonance': they need each other to achieve a certain goal. Your work benefits all group members; the work of the mates in your group benefits you. Students generally feel more responsibility in small groups than in larger ones.
- *Considerable promotive (face to face) interaction*: Group members help and encourage one another to learn. They have to be convinced that conversation, dialogue and exchange are needed to succeed, and they are given the space and time for face-to-face communication.
- *Individual accountability*: Each group member is responsible for contributing a fair share to the group's success and knows that they cannot 'hitchhike' on the work of others. This can be supported when students have different group roles.
- *Interpersonal and small group skills*: Group members have to develop skills with regard to communication, trust-building and conflict management, decision-making, and effective leadership. Teachers who pay explicit attention to the training of these skills, support students to become better 'group players'.
- *Group processing*: Students have the time and instruments to reflect on the quality of the group process regularly. Teachers can support this by regularly organizing group peer-evaluation sessions with accessible feedback tools (see chapter 7).

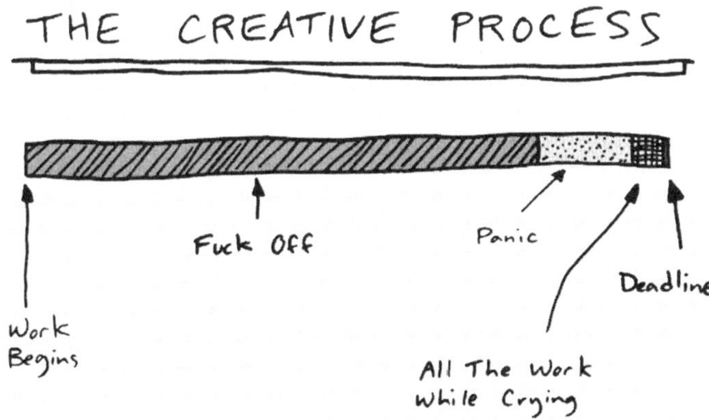

This drawing illustrates the emotional rollercoaster some people might experience during arts assignments

Guiding Creative Processes

Having to be instantly creative can confront students with 'blank page syndrome.' In his book *How to Write One Song*, musician Jeff Tweedy (of the band Wilco) states that rather than waiting for a 'divine intervention', usually 'inspiration has to be invited'.[36] To 'invite' inspiration, Tweedy uses exercises that help him to kickstart the creative process in a hands-on manner: freewriting, cutting up and remixing older texts, or stealing words or music from others.

Freewriting/-moving/-playing/-drawing/-filming exercises are a great medicine against a writer's block. Because there is usually a timer ticking, these exercises force students to produce a load of work in a short amount of time, postponing the critical reflection on the work's quality to a later moment.

One-Minute Drawings

Ronald Nijhof developed his *One-minute Powerpoint Drawing Assignments*, to help students to overcome an artist's block. On the basis of one-minute prompts on Powerpoint slides ('houseplant', 'clock'), each student produces 32 drawings in 32 minutes. Afterwards, the students sort all assignments: all clocks together, all houseplants, etc. After they have sorted all 32 drawings, students make a selection and mix the elements into new drawings that form the basis for new work.

Free drawing exercise

Students that do not know how to start may also need further guidance on aspects of their creative working process. For instance, they might not know what divergent thinking is or how to enhance it.[37] As a result, students can experience design fixation: they get stuck on a first idea for their arts assignment that is not necessarily an interesting one.[38] As a teacher, you can help your students by learning them the strategy to think up new ideas that are the opposite of their current idea, or by substituting one aspect for another.[39] More generally, research shows that it can help students if teachers pay explicit attention to different stages of a creative process, aiding them to comprehend and demystify this process.[40] Once students have started making, they can experience a whole range of feelings. Ojala and colleagues found that positive emotions (joy, curiosity, or a feeling of togetherness) during a (collaborative) creative process motivate students and can direct the making process forward.[41] However, negative emotions are just as common and can demotivate students, hampering their making process and reducing risk-taking. For instance, some students can feel overwhelmed by or uncomfortable with the relative openness of a Wicked Arts Assignment: they do not know when or how to start it or may be afraid of making mistakes.[42, 43] Students can also experience irritation, annoyance, anger, or disappointment when something takes too much time to make or when a result does not work out the way they want.[44] To help sustain the students' engagement and their persistence, it is important to validate both positive and negative emotions they may experience and aid them to tolerate negative ones, by helping them frame those feelings as a normal part of the creative working process.[45, 46]

Working with long-term Wicked Arts Assignments that span several weeks or months can confront students with problems, too. Seeing the amount of time they have, some overambitious students may want to set up a huge project, and you may need to assist them by scaling down their idea, concept, or narrative behind a work of art, sound sculpture, or artistic intervention.[47] Other students may linger or rush to finish their work—in both cases, it can be helpful to set very clear (intermediate) deadlines.

Procrastination is another problem that may arise with long term assignments. For example, students can keep on discussing ideas on end during lessons—without realizing any of them.[48] Yet, ideas can emerge from working with the materials of an arts assignment, not only from thinking or talking about ideas in advance. Students who keep on discussing (and disapproving!) ideas endlessly, can be helped if you provide them with materials from which ideas can emerge. What you will find is that certain properties of materials can elicit and encourage actions.[49] For instance, arts educator Maura Flood of the Art Institute of Chicago lays out materials in an attractive way, in what she calls a 'Materials Buffet', that inspires students to really get going! And if nothing helps, pull Andy Warhol's famous quote from your sleeve: 'Don't think about making art, just get it done. Let everyone else decide if it's good or bad ... While they are deciding, make even more art'.[50]

6.4 Designing Learning Activities for Your Curriculum

By now you have an overview of different learning activities, for different phases of your curriculum. Designing new learning activities is a creative act in itself. Experienced arts teachers often have a rich array of learning activities at their disposal, but how do you know which learning activity is in place? The rule of thumb here is that learning activities are means to achieve learning goals.[51] An attractive or playful learning activity that has no relation to any of the course's learning goals has little relevance for the student. So, the main design question here is: which learning activities support students to achieve the lessons' learning goals? Take a look at the learning goals you formulated (chapter 4), and ask yourself what kind of learning activity helps to realize each goal.

In your design, learning activities might be described as shown in the table below, with a learning goal, a time indication, and the learning activity. We admit that this way of describing your learning activities is time-consuming, but it adds to the transparency and transferability of your design, and it will cost you less time when you get more experienced. Furthermore, a thorough description helps you to share and exchange your best learning activities with colleagues!

Goal	Time	Learning Activity
Students can: • share and discuss different aspects of art and technology on the basis of recent articles	**10.00– 11.00**	**Sharing is caring** The class is divided into five groups. Every group has a different article on the subject 'art and technology', such as *Artistic Uses of Artificial Intelligence* or *Interactive Art*. Students first read the article individually (15 minutes), then make a summary in their expert group (20 minutes). Finally, they present their findings to the other students (25 minutes)

Learning activity *Sharing is caring*

6.5 The Building Blocks of Your Educational Design

After focusing on developing learning activities as building blocks for your curriculum, it's time to start building! You can combine your learning goals, chosen structure and developed learning activities in a lesson plan. The lesson plan gives you a sequenced overview of all the learning activities of your curriculum. It is up to you how detailed such an educational 'timetable' should look like. When teaching alone, a concise lesson plan can be sufficient. However, when more teachers are involved, or when teachers other than the designer have to implement the curriculum, a more elaborate plan is in order.

6.6 Design Result: Your Curriculum in Detail

By now you have filled in your curriculum in great detail. Based on your backbone curriculum you have:

- developed learning goals;
- chosen a structure;
- designed learning activities and checked if the student and teacher activities are varied and active enough;
- combined goals, structure and learning activities coherently in a lesson plan.

Like in other stages of the design process, revisions of decisions you made in earlier stages may be needed. The learning activities you designed might reveal that the time for every phase in your structure is too short or too long. Or you might discover that you need more, less, or clearer learning goals.

Phases Creative Process Model	Subgoals	Content/materials

Orientation phase	**Students can:**
	• research and discuss characteristics of superheroes in popular culture
	• discuss how contemporary artists use superheroes in a critical context
		Content
		• Comics: *Miss Fury*, *Superman*, *Batman*
		• Film/TV: *Black Panther*, *Super Sentai*, *Watchmen*
		• Art:
		  — Dara Birnbaum, *Technology Transformation: Wonder Woman*
		  — Dulce Pinzón, *La verdadera historia de los Superhéroes*
		
		Materials
		• post-its
		• laptops
		• projector

Research phase	**Students can:** • create a superhero with an unlikely 'superpower'	**Materials** • paper • markers

Lesson plan for one lesson of 120 minutes (first lesson of a series of six lessons)

Time	Learning Activity
09.00	**Vernacular superpowers** When entering class, students see the question: 'what is your (hidden) superpower?' on the wall. The students' vernacular 'super skills' (hula hooping, talking backwards, knowing every song of Rosalía by heart) are collected on post-its and stuck on the wall.
09.10	**Assignment** Explanation of the Wicked Arts Assignment: *Make a short movie about an unlikely superhero.*
09.20	**Super webquest** • The class is divided into six groups. Every group has to find information about an assigned superhero or supergroup (origin story, first and second identity, strong/weak points, societal role, 20 minutes). • They present their findings (max 3 minutes per group) with short discussion per example (30 minutes).
10.10	**Think-share-exchange** The works of Birnbaum and Pinzón are shown on the screen. For each work the teacher asks the (provocative) questions: • Which societal theme does this work touch on? • Do you feel that the artist criticizes the role of the superhero?
10.25	**Brainstorm in small groups** Students are divided in groups of 4–5. All groups are given a large piece of paper and markers. Question: inspired by the post-it we collected, write down different forms of skills that you find important, but that are usually not considered to be superpowers.
10.35	**Synthesizing** Create two different character descriptions based on the most interesting skills you collected.
10.55–11.00	**Summary and homework** Looking back and ahead to next week's lesson. Homework is announced: each group member collects background material and images of the 'superheroes' you created.

Next Up: Designing the Assessment of Learning

Now that we have discussed the most detailed building blocks of your educational design, let's return to one of the most essential questions of a curriculum. How can we see what our curriculum brings about? Chapter 7 will deal with the way students can be assessed in *Wicked Arts Education*, both during courses and projects as well as at the end.

NOTES

1   F. Hoobroeckx and E. M. Haak, *Onderwijskundig ontwerpen* [Educational Design] (Bohn Stafleu van Loghum, 2002).
2   S. Bertsch, B. J. Pesta, R. Wiscott and M. A. McDaniel, 'The Generation Effect: A Meta-Analytic Review', *Memory & Cognition*, 35 (2007), pp. 201–210.
3   L. Fiorella and R. E. Mayer, 'Eight Ways to Promote Generative Learning', *Educational Psychology Review*, 28 (2006), pp. 717–741.
4   M. Bremmer, E. Heijnen, A. Hotze, M. Pijls, E. Beamer, N. Roos, 'ArtsSciences Designathon: Solving Complex Problems in Interdisciplinary Teams', *European Journal of STEM Education*, 6(1), 11 (2021).
5   N. Kornell and R. A. Bjork, 'Learning concepts and categories: Is spacing the 'enemy of induction'?', *Psychol Sci*, 19(6) (2008), pp. 585–592.
6   T. Surma, K. Vanhoyweghen, D. Sluijsmans, G. Camp, D. Muijs and P. A. Kirschner, *Wijze lessen: Twaalf bouwstenen voor effectieve didactiek* [Valuable Lessons: Twelve Building Blocks for Effective Didactics] (Ten Brink Uitgevers, 2019).
7   G. Wiggins and J. McTighe, *Understanding by Design* (Association for Supervision and Curriculum Development ASCD, 2005).
8   W. Norsalawati, S. Bahrum, M. N. Ibrahim and H. Z. Hashim, 'Pedagogical Content Knowledge of Art Teachers in Teaching Visual Art Appreciation in School', *International Journal of Academic Research in Business and Social Sciences*, 7(12) (2017), pp. 296–303.
9   L. Fiorella and R. E. Mayer, 'Eight Ways to Promote Generative Learning', *Educational Psychology Review*, 28 (2016), pp. 717–741.
10 A. Paivio, *Imagery and Verbal Processes* (Holt, Rinehart and Winston, 1971).

11   R. E. Mayer, 'Multimedia Learning', *Psychology of Learning and Motivation*, 41 (2002), pp. 85–139.

12   R. E. Mayer, *Multimedia Learning*, 2nd edition (Cambridge University Press, 2009).

13   Wiley, 'Principles of Multimedia Learning', www.ctl.wiley.com/principles-of-multimedia-learning/

14   C. Bennett, '4 Fast Debate Formats for the Secondary Classroom' (2020), www.thoughtco.com/fast-debate-formats-for-the-classroom-8044.

15   T. Barrett, *Criticizing Art: Understanding the Contemporary* (McGraw-Hill, 2012).

16   VTS (Visual thinking strategies), www.vtshome.org/

17   A. Van Rensburg, 'Critical Thinking in Music' (Music Thinking Strategies), www.igniteart.weebly.com/music-thinking-strategies.html.

18   J. Lutters, 'Art-Based Learning', www.artez.nl/en/art-based-learning.

19   A. Van Rensburg, 'Critical Thinking in Music', www.igniteart.weebly.com/music-thinking-strategies.html.

20   D. Glass, A. Meyer and D. H. Rose, 'Universal Design for Learning and the Arts', *Harvard Educational Review*, 83(1) (2013), pp. 98–119.

21   Superuse Studio, 'Harvest! Collect! Re-use! The new building site', www.superuse-studios.com/de/publication/harvest-collect-re-use/.

22   R. K. Sawyer, *Group Genius: The Creative Power of Collaboration* (Basic Books, 2007).

23   J. New, *Drawing from Life: The Journal as Art* (Princeton Architectural Press, 2005).

24   Fiorella and Mayer, 'Eight Ways to Promote Generative Learning', *Educational Psychology Review*, 28 (2016), pp. 717–741.

25   J. Moon, *A Handbook of Reflective and Experiential Learning* (Routledge Falmer, 2004).

26   A. De la Croix and M. Veen, 'Wek reflectieve zombie tot leven!' [Bring the Reflective Zombie Back to Life], *Didactief*, 50(5) (2020), pp. 22–23.

27   DAS Theatre, 'Feedback Method' (2014), www.atd.ahk.nl/en/theatre-programmes/das-theatre/study-programme/feedback-method-1/.

28   Erasmus University Rotterdam, www.eur.nl/teacheur/one-minute-paper.

29   E. De Bono, *Six Thinking Hats: An Essential Approach to Business Management* (Little, Brown & Company, 1985).

30   M. Bremmer and E. Heijnen, 'Bridging Contradictions: The Design of Wicked Arts Assignments', in E. Heijnen and M. Bremmer (eds.), *Wicked Arts Assignments* (Valiz, 2020), pp. 23–32.

31   P. A. Kirschner, J. Sweller and R. E. Clark, 'Why Minimal Guidance During Instruction Does Not Work: An Analysis of the Failure of Constructivist, Discovery, Problem-Based, Experiential, and Inquiry-Based Teaching', *Educational Psychologist*, 41(2) (2006), pp. 75–86.

32   T. Surma, K. Vanhoyweghen, D. Sluijsmans, G. Camp, D. Muijs and P. A. Kirschner, *Wijze lessen: Twaalf bouwstenen voor effectieve didactiek* [Valuable Lessons: Twelve Building Blocks for Effective Didactics] (Ten Brink Uitgevers, 2019).

33   K. Dirkx, J. Hubertina, G. Camp, L. Kester and P. Kirschner, 'Do Secondary School Students Make Use of Effective Study Strategies When They Study on Their Own?', *Applied Cognitive Psychology*, 33(5) (2019), pp. 1–6.

34   R. Pauli, C. Mohiyeddini, D. Bray, F. Michie and B. Street, 'Individual Differences in Negative Group Work Experiences in Collaborative Student Learning', *Educational Psychology*, 28(1) (2008), pp. 47–58.

35   D. W. Johnson, R. T. Johnson and E. Holubec, *The New Circles of Learning: Cooperation in the Classroom and School* (The Association for Supervision and Curriculum Development, 1994).

36   J. Tweedy, *How to Write One Song* (Faber & Faber, 2020), p. 17.

37   M-Th. A. Van de Kamp, *Reimagine, Redesign and Transform: Enhancing Generation and Exploration in Creative Problem Finding Processes in Visual Arts Education*, Ph.D. diss. (Universiteit van Amsterdam, 2017).

38   B. Nicholl and R. McLellan, 'The Contribution of Product Analysis to Fixation in Students' Design and Technology Work', in E.W.L. Norma and D. Spendlove (eds.), *The Design and Technology Association International Research Conference 2007* (The Design and Technology Association, 2017), pp. 71–76.

39   R. K. Sawyer, 'Teaching and Learning How to Create in Schools of Art and Design', *Journal of the Learning Sciences*, 27(1) (2018), pp. 137–181.

40   T. Groenendijk, *Observe and Explore: Empirical Studies About Learning in Creative Writing and the Visual Arts*, Ph.D. diss. (Universiteit van Amsterdam, 2012).

41   M. Ojala, S. Karppinen and E. Syrjäläinen, 'Toward Making Sense of Self Through Emotional Experiences in Craft-Art', *Craft Research*, 9(2) (2018), pp. 201–227.

42   J. L. Miraglia, *Conceptions of Art: A Case Study of Elementary Teachers, a Principal, and an Art Teacher*, Ph.D. diss. (University of Massachusetts, 2006).

43   R. K. Sawyer, 'Teaching and Learning How to Create in Schools of Art and Design', *Journal of the Learning Sciences*, 27(1) (2018), pp. 137–181.

44   M. Ojala, S. Karppinen and E. Syrjäläinen, 'Toward Making Sense of Self Through Emotional Experiences in Craft-Art'.

45   E. Winner, *An Uneasy Guest in the Schoolhouse: Art Education from Colonial Times to a Promising Future* (Oxford University Press, 2022).

46   G. Claxton, *Wise-Up: The Challenge of Lifelong Learning* (Bloomsbury, 1999).

47   R. K. Sawyer, 'Teaching and Learning How to Create in Schools of Art and Design', *Journal of the Learning Sciences*, 27(1) (2018), pp. 137–181.

48   M. Bremmer, E. Heijnen, A. Hotze, M. Pijls, E. Beamer and N. Roos, 'ArtsSciences Designathon: Solving Complex Problems in Interdisciplinary Teams', *European Journal of STEM Education*, 6(1) (2021), p. 11.

49   M. Hoekstra, 'Artist teachers and Democratic Pedagogy', unpublished Ph.D. diss. (University of Chester, 2018).

50   P. Brown, 'Catholicism and Commercialism: The Many Aspects of Andy Warhol's Life', *Clio: WVU Art History Research Journal*, 1(1), (2021), p. 27.

51   F. Hoobroeckx and E. M. Haak, *Onderwijskundig ontwerpen*.

Chapter 7

Assessment of Students' Learning

Amateur Night in the Apollo Theater in Harlem is America's longest running talent show, and once launched the careers of Ella Fitzgerald, James Brown, The Jackson Five and Lauryn Hill, and others. Contestants are vocalists, rappers, dancers, comedians, spoken-word artists and other performers. For some of them the audience will cheer and show their 'Yass!!' signs, but often the tough audience will call for their removal by booing and showing their 'Boo!!' signs. In that case, the 'executioner' will relentlessly sweep performers off the stage. Finally, only one of the contestants will be taking home the Amateur Night Grand Prize.

Yass or Boo is a very crude form of assessment, even for a talent show. Contrary to this, in arts education many teachers are reluctant to make assessments, or even reject them.[1] Stereotypically, the arts are associated with creativity and unique personal qualities and taste, whereas assessment is associated with standards and comparability. Yet, contests, critics, and juries are quite common in the arts world, and in education assessment is much more than grading or pass-or-fail decisions. Assessment is inherent to teaching and learning. It helps us to answer crucial questions such as 'are we teaching what we think we are teaching', and 'are students learning what we think they are learning?'

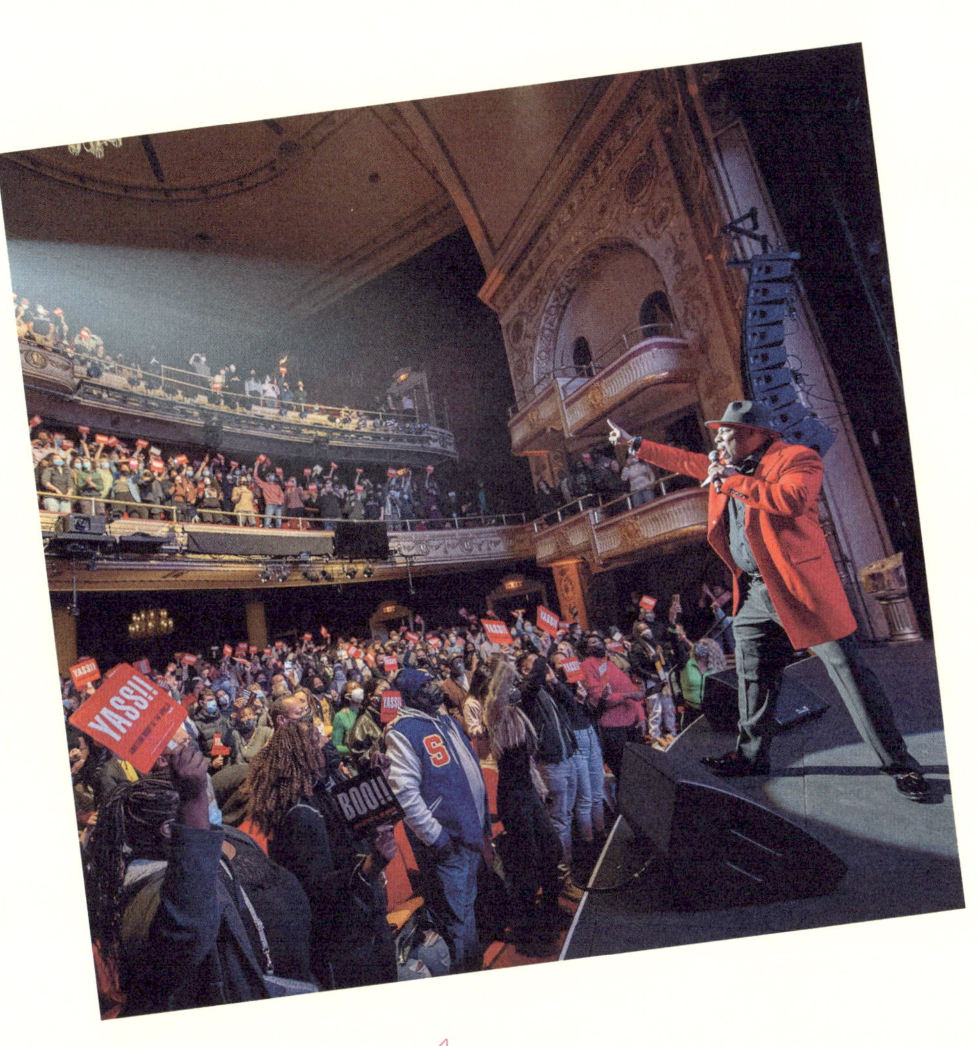

Apollo Theater, Amateur Night (2019)

Contents of this chapter

7.1 Assessing Wicked Arts Assignments

Assessment is the process by which information is gathered to monitor the progress of student learning and to analyse the learning outcomes. It helps planning future teaching and provides evidence of achievement to the students and to the wider community. Many will recognize that the somewhat shady reputation of assessment among arts educators often has to do with its association with 'old school' tests. Short-answer or multiple-choice tests are suitable for traditional frontal classroom instruction and learning facts, but a total mismatch for assessing the quality of, say, a creative process. So, alignment between learning goals, learning activities, and assessment is crucial.[2]

Before you can start designing your assessments you have to answer a number of questions: Why do you assess? What do you assess? Which form of assessment do you choose? How do you interpret the outcomes? Who does the assessment? Who is assessed? Where do you assess?

Wicked Arts Education calls for authentic forms of assessment. These assessments show how well students apply their knowledge, skills, and abilities to realistic problems in the arts. We will present answers to the assessment questions in relation to Wicked Arts Assignments, but in some cases our answers can be applied to all kinds of education.

7.2 Why Do You Assess?

Summative and Formative Assessment

Assessment can serve various functions in arts education. A major distinction is between summative assessment (assessment *of* learning) and formative assessment (assessment *for* learning.

The main question of summative assessment is: did the students actually learn what they were expected to learn? Summative assessments usually occur at the end of a project or course or a number of lessons. They tend to result in quantitative measures, such as a grade or a scale score, and are used for pass-or-fail decisions.

Formative assessment aims at improving student learning.[3] Here, the main question is diagnostic in character: what are strengths and weaknesses of the students' work and what feedback can improve their learning? Formative assessments take place during a lesson or course and give teachers the opportunity to adapt their teaching. Thus, it provides students with strategies on how to bridge their 'learning gap': the gap between their performance and the desired learning goals.

In arts education, summative and formative assessment are often combined. For instance, summative assessments can have formative aspects, when grades or scores are accompanied by teachers' comments and feedback.

Feedback

The information provided by a teacher, peer, or expert regarding aspects of a student's performance is generally called feedback. Hattie and Timperley distinguish three forms of feedback that, taken together, enhance the learning process: feedup, feedback and feedforward.[4]

Teachers can start their course or project with feedup, answering the question for students: *where am I going?* The aim of feed-up is that they understand the main learning goals and assessment criteria. During the course, feedback can be given to students, answering the question: *how am I going?* Feedback can be aimed at cognitive processes, for example proposing alternative strategies to find creative solutions. But it also can be aimed at motor skills e.g. optimizing dance moves or touch on the keys, or at affective processes, e.g. increasing motivation or engagement. Feedback does not always have to be verbal. In the performing arts non-verbal feedback can be applied during a rehearsal of a performance by means of gestures, body positioning and physical actions of the teacher. Feedforward, finally, answers the question for students: *where to go next?* It is closely related to feedback, but its emphasis is more on the future. Here the aim is to answer questions like: what else do you need to work on and how are you going to do that?

Feedback can be delivered to and received by both individuals and groups. To be effective, feedback should be geared toward the appropriate level of the students, and related to important dimensions of the Wicked Arts Assignment. Therefore, tips and tops that are not directed to the attainment of the learning goals can be confusing.

Moreover, feedback should be directed at the learning achievement, not at the person.[5] As in the arts, the products and performances can be highly personal and students can feel vulnerable when critical feedback is given. Most teachers realize that and try to find a balance between critique and encouragement.

7.3 What Do You Assess?

The very first thing you will do when you think about the *what* of assessment, is to return to your learning goals. Learning goals ideally reflect what students (should) have learned during your lesson, course, or project, and therefore form the basis of any assessment. You do not need to assess every learning goal, but will decide for every course or project which ones are necessary to assess.

Within *Wicked Arts Education*, the content of the learning goals will always be related to the central Wicked assignment(s), often complemented with other goals referring to, for example, arts theory, arts reception or presenting. So, the one thing you will certainly assess is the students' performance of the Wicked Arts Assignment. Although this seems quite obvious, there are some choices to be made when assessing this type of assignment.

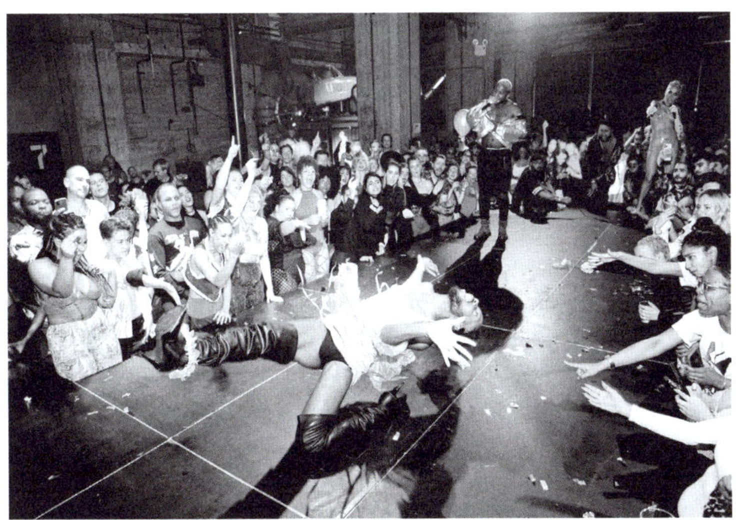

Naomi He-Ji, *Once Upon a Ball* (2021). 'Stop vagueing and start voguing'. In the Ballroom-scene, assessment plays an important role. On the runway, performers are judged based on categories such as 'Realness with a twist', 'Bizarre', and 'Sex Siren'

Process and/or Product

Are you going to assess final results or is the process of how those
results were achieved more important? The product-oriented
approach evaluates the outcome of the learning process, whereas the
process-oriented approach evaluates the process itself. Assessment
need not be either process- or product-oriented, but can encompass
both. For instance, you could include criteria for the way a composition sounds and for the compositional process.

Holistic or Separate Criteria?

It might seem attractive to assess a Wicked Arts Assignment
as an integrated whole. This is called holistic assessment, for
instance in the form of one overall grade for an assignment. Yet,
for students it is more insightful when you design a set of specific
criteria that assess different aspects of an achievement, such as
products, *processes* and *arts reception*.

When you assess the result of a Wicked Arts Assignment
you can think of criteria concerning technical skills, expression,
interpretation, and communication, such as: is the form of the
product or performance appropriate to communicate the ideas of
the student? When a process is assessed, you might assess aspects
such as problem setting, doing research, developing ideas,
experimenting with different solutions, taking risks, sharing
ideas, or self-reflection.

If you are assessing arts reception, you can think of criteria
concerning description of style and genre, historical and social
contexts, function and meaning in artistic work, if a student can
take different perspectives on an artwork, or can substantiate
how they experience an artwork.

Using separate and detailed criteria may positively affect
student performance, reduce their anxiety and support learning.
On the other hand, too detailed criteria may have a limiting
influence on the autonomy and creativity of the student.

7.4 Which Form of Assessment Do You Choose?

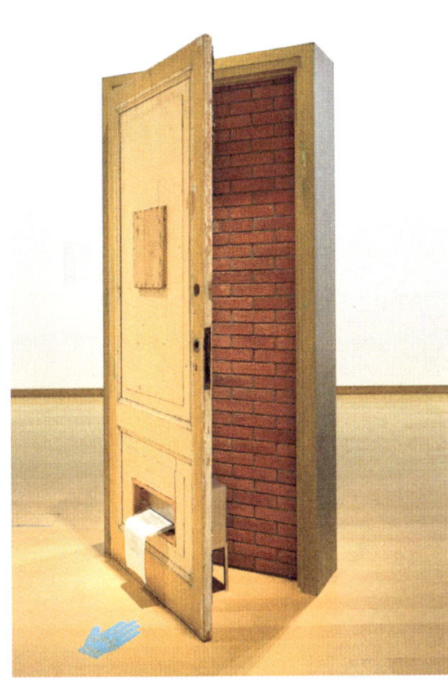

Ghita Skali, *Relentless Putridity* (2023). In the early twentieth century, nominees for the prestigious art prize Prix de Rome were confined behind closed doors to take an exam. Arts materials and meals were provided through a hatch. By exposing one of the original doors in front of a brick wall, Skali criticizes the exclusive selection process of art prizes up to today

As soon as you have decided what you will assess and why, the next thing you will think about is the form of the assessment. Summative assessments can take on a variety of forms. We are all familiar with tests and exams, formats that were even used to select the winner of renowned arts prizes, as Ghita Skali's critical work *Relentless Putridity* illustrates. Presentations, performances, research reports, or projects that demonstrate the knowledge and skills a student has learned are often more in place in arts educational contexts.

Formative assessments can vary from very informal to more structured forms. They can range from incidental comments as a regular part of classwork, to structured feedback, interviews, and reports. A general recommendation is that you should use choice and flexibility in assessment forms wherever possible. Furthermore, you should provide support and training for any new skills or technologies that will be used in assessments.

The same assessment form can sometimes be both summative and formative.[6] A much used example for formative and summative assessment is the so-called 'rubric', which seems applicable within *Wicked Arts Education*.

Rubric

Because the students' performance of a Wicked Arts Assignment is multifaceted and often needs a more complex form of assessment, a rubric can be a suitable form. A rubric is an assessment tool that consists of a criteria list *and* descriptions of different performance levels for each criterion.[7,8] As both criteria and descriptions of levels are described, a rubric offers students much insight into what is expected. Furthermore, one rubric can contain both criteria for the learning process and the product.

An example of part of a rubric is presented in the table below. It contains two criteria derived from learning goals that refer to researching during a creative process: collecting sources of inspiration and experimenting.

Criteria	Levels			
	1	2	3	4
Collecting sources of inspiration	You collected almost no sources of inspiration and you did not study (e.g. by sketches or notes) a theme to work on.	You collected a few sources of inspiration to study (e.g. by sketches or notes) a preliminary theme to work on.	You made an extensive collection of sources of inspiration to study (e.g. by sketches or notes) one theme in depth to work on.	You made an extensive and varied collection of sources of inspiration to study (e.g. by sketches or notes) several themes in depth to work on.
Experimenting	You started directly to produce your final product. You did not try out different concepts, materials, techniques or methods.	You took a little time experimenting. You tried one or two concepts, materials, techniques or methods, but it is unclear how this relates to your final work.	You took time experimenting. You tried out several concepts, materials, techniques or methods, which helped you to create your final work.	You took a lot of time experimenting. You tried out a broad range of concepts, materials, techniques or methods, as well as unusual possibilities, resulting in discoveries you used in your final work.

Example of part of a rubric for researching during a creative process (based on Groenendijk[9])

In this rubric, the performance levels are 1 (unsatisfactory), 2 (partially proficient), 3 (proficient) and 4 (advanced). However, you can also opt for three performance levels: ranging from 0 (below level) to 1 (at level) and 2 (above level). Or you could choose a five-point scale or use even more levels, but this makes it difficult to provide descriptions of the different levels that are clearly distinguishable from each other. The disadvantage of three or five levels is that assessors can be tempted to choose the neutral level in the middle, whereas an even number of levels forces assessors to make a choice.

As mentioned earlier, rubrics can be used for both formative and summative assessment. Regarding formative assessment, a rubric is a form of feedup, showing students in the beginning of a course where they will be going. Rubrics can also be used for providing feedback during the course and help inform feeding forward: What needs to be undertaken to make further progress? Yet, rubrics can just as easily be used for summative assessment, providing students with a grade.

Rubrics can be either specific or general. Assignment-specific rubrics are easier to score, as criteria are closely related to the content and process of a certain assignment. General rubrics, however, enable students to monitor their progress over different assignments. The rubric is a general rubric, because the criteria can be used in different assignments that involve designing creative products.

To provide more room for personal feedback for a student, a text field could be added in a rubric. Furthermore, if you think that there is a quality in the achievement that is not adequately described in the criteria, you can build in an 'escape criterion'. This criterion can be called the 'wow or X factor', assessing the intangible qualities of an artistic achievement. But you should be sparse with such escapes, as frequent use interferes with the transparency of the assessment.

Visual Rubric for (Self-)Assessment

Arts educators Maarleveld and Kortland[10] developed a visual rubric system in which pictures represent the criteria and students can mark or colour these to indicate their attained levels. Besides for self-assessments, the visual rubric can also be used for peer-assessment and, for instance, the results can be compared with the teacher's assessment.

A visual rubric might make (self-)assessment easier and more attractive. Because it is both text- and picture-based, it provides students with multiple representations of criteria.

For instance, the pictures in their rubric were made on the basis of texts describing the criteria and the performance levels. The texts concerning two criteria, namely *Collecting sources of inspiration* and *Experimenting* were visually translated. Of course, the same criterion can be 'translated' into different pictures.

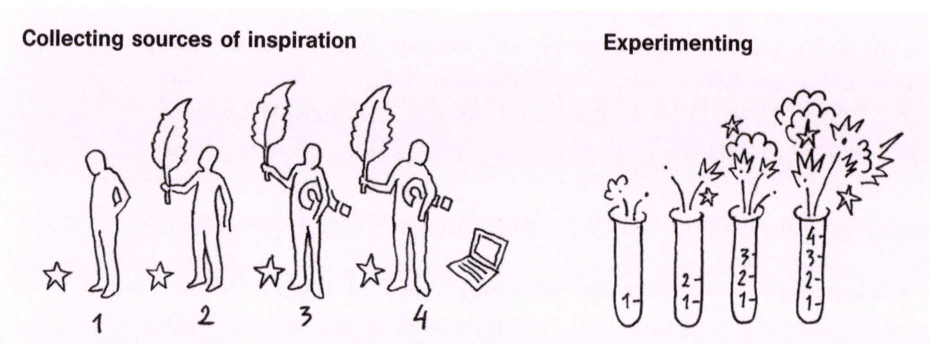

Criteria of *Collecting sources of inspiration* and *Experimenting* (based on Maarleveld & Kortland, 2013)[11]

The Hungarian researchers Kárpáti and Paál used visual rubrics to assess theatre lessons and one of their criteria concerning collaboration can be used for assessing different arts disciplines (see figure on the next page).[12]

Wicked Arts Education

Acting performance

How did you perform the play through your mimics, body language and voice?

Assessment of artistic competencies through visual rubrics[13]

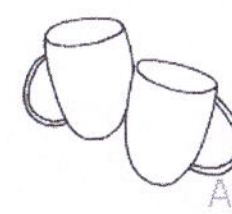
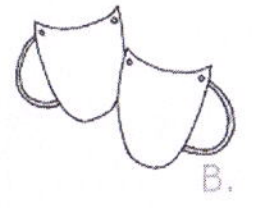
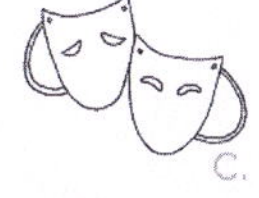

Directing

How did you realise team management and direct play in line with your intentions?

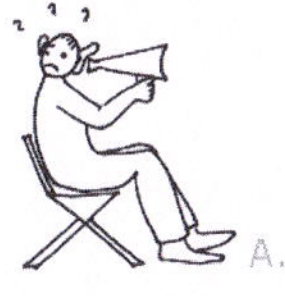
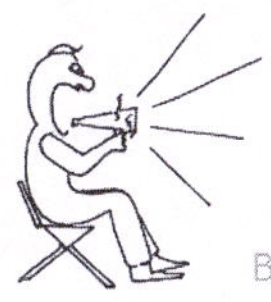
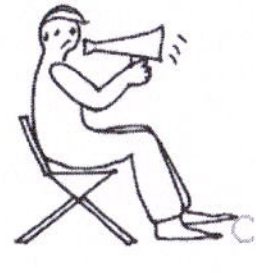
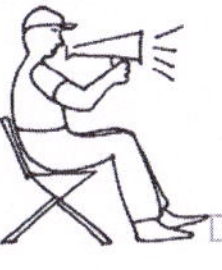

Collaboration

How is your participation in group work?

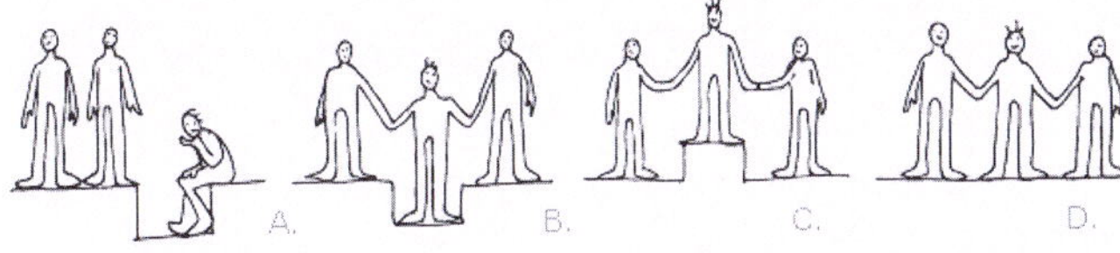

Research on visual rubrics shows they can be successfully employed.[14, 15] Students are positive about the pictures and say it helps them to understand learning goals and assessment criteria. Teachers say it helps them to have feedback conversations with students. Although visual rubrics are attractive, they are not without problems. The teacher has to explain and discuss the meaning of the visual rubrics carefully with the students. Furthermore, symbolic pictures can be confusing to some students because they take them literally. For instance, the image for *Collecting sources of inspiration* can evoke the question: why does that person hold a leaf?

In the Appendix (pp. 174–181) you can find both a visual and textual rubric that is general (intended to assess different assignments) and can be used in all arts disciplines or interdisciplinary projects. It contains criteria concerning *Arts Appreciation*, *Research*, *Arts Production*, *Presentation and Performance*. You can make use of these rubrics, but we also suggest designing innovative rubrics for your specific contexts! Both with visual and textual rubrics, the construction is an ongoing process of implementation and revision.

Portfolio Assessment

Portfolios provide ways of assessing students' learning over time. In the arts, portfolios often form a collection of someone's best achievements, meant for presentation and evaluation by external audiences. In education, however, portfolios can have different forms and purposes.

Portfolios come in many forms, from physical collections of student work that include materials such as written assignments, compositions, sketches and artworks to online digital archives and websites created by students. Online portfolios (also called *digital portfolios* or *e-portfolios*) can feature photos or videos of the same materials as physical portfolios, but may also include other digital artifacts of learning, such as performances.

Portfolios can also have different purposes. They can provide insight into what students created (product-based portfolio), or provide insight in how and why they created it (process-based portfolio). The latter means that the portfolio not only contains student's pieces of work, but also reflective and explanatory written data. A process-based portfolio can also illustrate learning through multiple forms and media such as research, experiments, try-outs, and sketches, like an artist's journal. Also, process-based portfolio blogs or online journals may show ongoing reflections about learning activities, progress, and accomplishments.

Portfolios usually contain rich information for assessment, but the process of collecting, selecting, reflecting, presenting, and discussing is laborious for both students and teachers. Clear agreements must be made about the nature and quantity of the content. Ideally, the portfolio should be as student-centred as possible and the role of the teacher is to facilitate and guide putting together the portfolio. But it is possible that the teacher determines which results of assignments should be part of it. For instance, when the portfolio is used for providing evidence for a grade, then all students should provide some standard work in their portfolios. There can also be combinations of teacher and student responsibility concerning the content of the portfolio. Individual choice and autonomy in putting together a portfolio will be engaging for students, and in some cases students might also be given total ownership of the portfolio.

Clear agreements must also be made about the function of the assessment and the criteria and performance levels that will be employed. Portfolios can be used for summative assessment as well as formative assessment, such as self-reflection, self-assessment and for diagnosing learning needs. Rubrics should be used in order to determine the quality of the evidence in a portfolio and to make a reliable and valid assessment.

Do note that presenting and discussing the portfolio takes time, but this form of assessment is educationally effective only when it is done thoroughly. Discussion and giving feedback and feedforward can be limited to the teacher and student, but often involves fellow students. Portfolios may also be presented to parents and community members as part of a demonstration of learning.

Even though the portfolio has its origins in the visual arts, it is now used in other arts disciplines as well. Dunbar-Hall and colleagues[16] mention the ability of portfolios 'to address the specific nature of dance and music as performative, creative, and representational arts by collating in one location multiple forms of digital information — audio recordings, video footage, and digitized documents and graphics'.[17] An example for music education is presented below.

Example: Music Portfolio

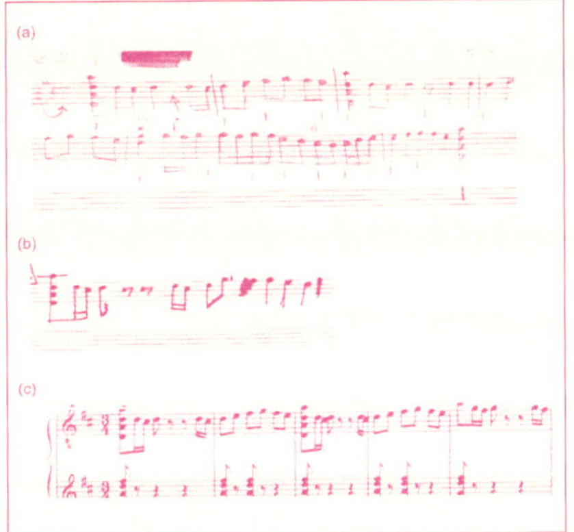

By incorporating performing, creating, and responding into the music portfolio, students can provide a demonstration of their musical growth over time. This student portfolio excerpt is based on Silveira and contains recording rehearsals of the same piece at different times in the course.[18] From melodic (a) and rhythmic (b) sketches to an excerpt of the final notated form (c). After each recording, students can complete a rehearsal critique and teachers assess the critique against a rubric. The portfolio can also contain composition assignments and examples of describing and analysing different musical genres.

7.5 How to Interpret Assessment Outcomes?

Assessment shows evidence of learning, but this evidence can be interpreted in different ways. Is evidence of learning based on a comparison with the criteria formulated for a lesson or course (criterion-referenced) or is it based on a comparison with other students (norm-referenced)? This means knowing a student's result for a criterion-referenced assessment will tell you how that specific student performed in relation to the criterion, but not whether they performed below-average, above-average, or average compared to their peers like norm-referenced assessment will indicate.

Criterion-referenced and norm-referenced assessments can be mixed. For instance, when you have established performance levels of individual students in relation to your criteria, it is natural and useful to look at all the students' results in total. If the majority of students do not attain a minimum performance level on certain criteria, this is a cause for further analysis. Is the criterion not related to the learning goal or does the teaching of this goal need to be changed?

Another option is that two students may have the same grade, but based on your holistic assessment (or gut feeling), you think one performance is better than the other. Then you go back to assessments of the different criteria in the rubrics of these two students, and try to find the cause of this. Perhaps a certain criterion was assessed too low or too high. Or perhaps it is the 'wow factor' that makes the difference. Or perhaps you must conclude that you were a bit prejudiced and expected student A to perform better than B. Such a comparison can result in a good correction.

Criteria and rubrics should demonstrate how a student has performed during a course or project, but they do not show whether a student has improved compared to a previous performance. Looking at both the student's earlier work and their current work is used in many informal learning communities (see for example Deviant Art, top right). Students who feel that they have progressed during the course or compared to an earlier course, but are not yet meeting the goals may become discouraged or demotivated. Hughes thinks that comparing past and present work provides formative feedback about a student's current progress, rather than what is lacking to meet the criteria and (rubric) performance levels required at the end of a course.[19] Students might become more motivated through focusing on achievable performance levels and this might raise their self-esteem. Another way to motivate students is by asking them to formulate their own learning goals, as mentioned in 3.5.

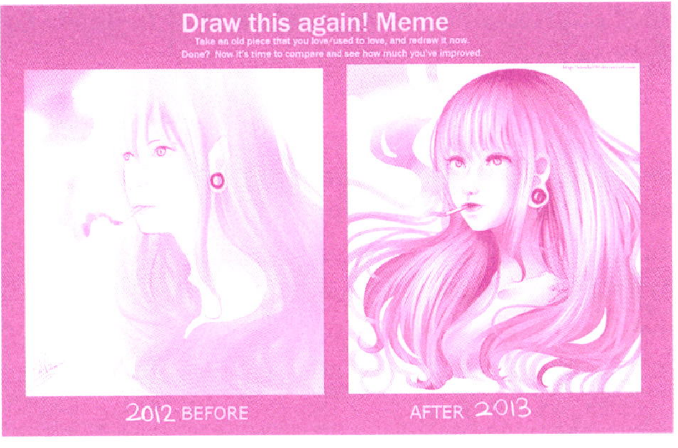

Example of *Draw this Again* on the website Deviant Art

7.6   Who Does the Assessment?

Teacher

A teacher has many roles in education and one important role is that of assessor. A teacher's knowledge and skills to plan and implement different forms of assessment, to interpret evidence and outcomes of summative or formative assessment, and to engage students as participants in assessment of their own learning, are all part of a teacher's assessment literacy.[20] Just like curriculum design and teaching, assessment needs not be a solitary practice, but it can be a collaborative endeavour. Planning and executing assessment in collaboration with colleagues can be helpful to reduce individual bias of teachers and can raise the reliability of assessment.

Student

Not only teachers can assess students' learning, students themselves can do so, too. Sluijsmans et al.[21] describe self-assessment as one method of formative assessment. It is important that students learn to assess their own work in arts education because it fosters learner autonomy. Artists engage in self-assessment continuously[22] and this regulates and stimulates their artistic process and learning in art. Lindström[23] also considers the capacity for self-assessment important in the art making process and suggests it could be a criterion that art teachers use in assessing their students.

Ross[24] suggests that even though a substantial number of teachers use self-assessment, they have doubts about the value and accuracy of this method. For instance, teachers think that good students underestimate their work whereas underachievers often overestimate compared to the teacher's assessments. Research into self-assessment in art education indicates that this is not necessarily so.[25] Differences in assessment occur because students can have other interpretations of assessment criteria than their teachers. Therefore, training students to assess their work may increase agreement between self-assessment scores and teacher scores.

Ross[26] lists four ways to train students to improve their self-assessments: (1) involve students in the definition of criteria, (2) instruct them how to apply them, (3) provide feedback on the outcomes of self-assessment, (4) help students plan their activities based on assessment results. The outcomes of self-assessment of a student can be compared to the outcomes of teacher- or peer-assessment of that student.

Peers

Peer-assessment is often connected to self-assessment, but is used less frequently.[27] Peer-assessment can stimulate involvement in the assessment and can lead to better understanding of assessment criteria as students express the criteria in their own words while communicating with peers.[28] Peer-assessment is most appropriate for formative assessment, as summative assessment between peers may lead to conflicts of loyalty. Peer-assessment is possible in elementary education, but more common in secondary education.

The format for peer-assessment can be general and open or tailored to a specific assignment, for example a monologue presentation in theatre lessons (see modelling sheet on the next page).

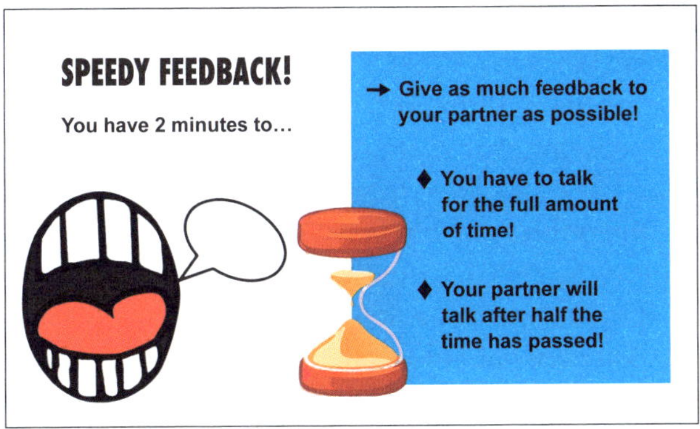

Open format for peer assessment on Theartteacher.net

Peer Evaluation Modelling Sheet

Name: ....
Partner: ....

In pairs, watch each other's monologue and then respond to each question.

What am I looking for in this monologue?
Examples:
- 'it's memorized'
- 'a strong character'
- 'performance is committed and focused'

What did my partner do?
Examples:
- 'the monologue was memorized'
- 'they had a great character'
- 'they sat in a chair the whole time'
- 'they were really into the performance'

What can my partner remember for next time?
Examples:
- 'Try moving more, it fits the piece to have the character be more active'
- 'There was a lot of yelling, maybe try for a quiet moment?'
- 'You were totally in character!'

Peer evaluation modelling sheet for theatre education with examples of feedback[29]

Experts

Wicked Arts Education strives for meaningful and realistic forms of learning and evaluation. An assessment is realistic when it resembles the complexity of real-life situations, for instance during a group critique in the context of a public performance or exhibition. Sometimes assignments are suited to give external experts (performers, artists, art critics, etc.) a role in providing feedback. It is important to establish in advance what this role is. In general, the teacher remains responsible for final summative assessments, because the teacher has the formal authority to teach and to assess.

7.7 Who Is Assessed?

Assessment does not always concern individual students. When an assignment requires group work, which it often does in *Wicked Arts Education*, and the group submits one product or performance the question is whether all group members should receive the same assessment. That is the easiest solution. However, when individual contributions are not reflected in the assessments, stronger students may be disadvantaged by weaker ones and vice versa. There are a number of solutions for this problem:

- Each student is given an allocated task that contributes to the final group product and will be assessed for that task. The difficulty is to find tasks that are equal in size and complexity. Moreover, this way of assessing may not encourage collaboration. Therefore, one could assess the individual contributions as well as the group product as a whole.
- If allocated tasks are not feasible, one could give a group assessment and ask students to demonstrate their learning. This can be accomplished through individual records of the learning process. Especially if collaboration is a learning goal and a criterion to be assessed, you are dependent on self- and peer-assessment. You can ask students to evaluate the group's dynamics and the contributions of the students themselves and their teammates. Criteria can be the degree of participation, communication skills, taking responsibility, adaptability and the like.

Example: Bandcheck

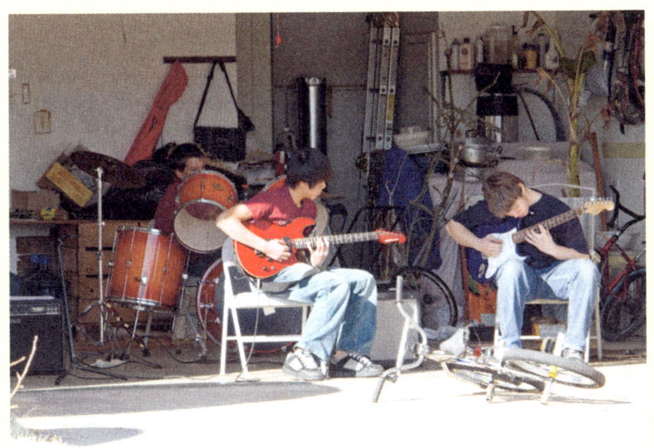

Garage band rehearsal space

Singing, playing and improvising in friendship groups are important in music learning outside school. According to Green, music education should make use of these kinds of informal learning practices.[30] This entails that the assessment needs to consider assessment of musical collaboration and musical interactions in groups.

Bandcheck, developed by Van Hoek,[31] is a tool that aims at assessing musical communication in school bands in secondary education. It distinguishes three modes that constitute musical communication: listening, looking, and moving. Listening concerns being aware of how the music is played or sung by oneself and the other members of the band. But it also concerns being aware of the oral feedback that is provided during music making. Looking concerns being aware of oneself and of the others, and moving concerns being aware of nonverbal cues, such as hand gestures, nodding of the head and stamping of the feet. These three modes have four levels: (1) basic level: self-directed, (2) occasionally being aware of the others, (3) being able to observe the others (4) being able to anticipate.

After a rehearsal the members of the band can assess themselves, but also peer-assessment and assessment by the teacher are possible. Bandcheck is an interactive webtool and the results are saved and can be shown to the band as a total. This makes it suitable for formative assessment in giving feedback and stimulating feedforward.

Assessing musical collaboration and interaction

7.8   Where Do You Assess?

Physical Context

Assessments in real-life contexts should take social and physical context into account. For instance, assessments could take place in museums, studios, or theatres. The physical context also concerns the availability of resources (instruments, tools, props, etc.) that are needed to meet the requirements of an assignment.

Digital Context

Internet can also qualify as context for assessment. In social media people assess and are assessed continuously through numbers of hits, likes, followers, reviews, etc. Striving for the most likes is hardly educationally relevant (although: see example *Internet Famous*), but getting reviews from peers outside school can be an additional form of formative assessment.

Example: Internet Famous

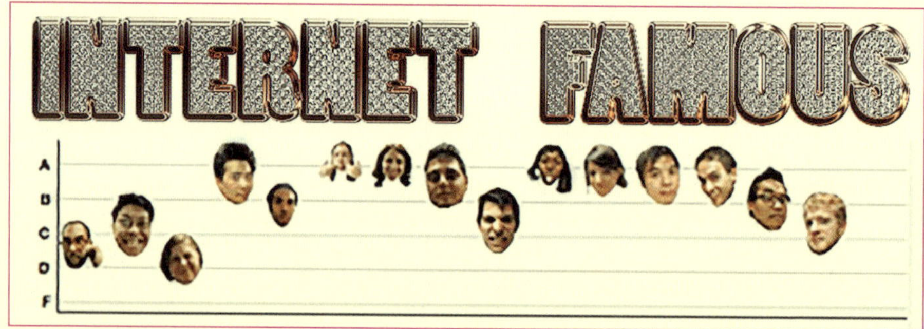

James Powderly, Evan Roth & Jamie Wilkinson, *Internet Famous* (2007–2008)

At Parsons, the New York City design school, the artists Evan Roth and James Powderly and software developer Jamie Wilkinson created *Internet Famous*, a course to learn how to use the rules guiding online commerce. The motive was that online strategies for distributing and promoting their art are essential tools for twenty-first-century artists. The course was graded by algorithm: by analysing a number of sites a software tool assigns each student a 'Famo Index Score' that determines each grade.

7.9 The Quality of Assessment

Just like teaching, the assessments of students' learning can differ in quality. Not all feedback is effective and not all summative assessment is fair. Four important quality features are reliability, validity, transparency, and practicality.

Assessments should be reliable. Reliability refers to the consistency of an assessment. First of all, consistency over time: will teachers with little time come to the same result in comparison to a week later if they have more time and are more relaxed? Secondly, a reliable assessment is also consistent across different teachers. So, two colleagues should come to the same result, or at least there should not be a substantial difference between grades. This demands that the criteria and assessment procedures must be clearly formulated, and not be subject to different interpretations.

Assessment instruments should be valid. Validity of an assessment is related to whether an assessment measures what it is supposed to measure. A valid assessment covers the goals of the lesson or curriculum and does not assess criteria that were unknown at the start or that are irrelevant for the assignment. A reliable measurement is not always valid: the results might be reproducible, but they are not necessarily correctly representing what they are supposed to assess. A simple example: when assessing the process of making a visual product or writing a song one could just count the number of sketches or the number of recorded drafts. This is a reliable assessment: a teacher will make the same assessment now and a week later and two colleagues will come to the same assessment. However, just counting the number of sketches or drafts is a very limited assessment of the working process. A valid assessment pays attention to different aspects of the process, such as doing research, experimenting with different solutions, and taking risks.

Assessments should be transparent. Transparency involves explicit criteria and standards to make sure that students know how the assessment works. It also involves that the assessment procedure is clear. For instance, when peers or experts are involved, it should be known in advance what their role will be and to what extent their judgements will be taken into account.

Lastly, assessment should be practicable, that is constructing the assessment and making the judgements should be feasible in the time available for the teacher. For instance, creating and maintaining student portfolios can be time-consuming. So even when they can be a valid and valuable form of assessment, teachers may find that portfolios are not a feasible option.

7.10 Design Result: Your Curriculum's Assessment Methods

By now you know that student assessment is part of teaching and learning. You can choose whether your assessment is formative or summative, product- or process-oriented or both, what is an adequate assessment form, and how to interpret assessment outcomes. You decide whether, apart from you as a teacher, others will take part in the assessment: students themselves, their peers, or experts. Lastly, but not unimportantly: check the quality of the assessment!

Next Up: Curriculum Evaluation

You now have designed all aspects of your curriculum, but curriculum design does not stop here. When the curriculum is implemented, you want to know if it works as intended. So, you need to evaluate it. The last chapter deals with ways in which you can carry out the evaluation of your curriculum.

Wicked Arts Education

NOTES

1 E. Soep, 'Assessment and Visual Arts Education', in E. W. Eisner and M. D. Day (eds.), *Handbook of Research and Policy in Art Education* (Lawrence Erlbaum Publishers, 2004), pp. 579–583.

2 J. T. M. Gulikers, T. J. Bastiaens and P. A. Kirschner, 'A Five-Dimensional Framework for Authentic Assessment', *Educational Technology Research and Development*, 52(3) (2004), pp. 67–86.

3 S. M. Brookhart, 'Successful Students' Formative and Summative Uses of Assessment Information', *Assessment in Education: Principles, Policy and Practice*, 8(2) (2001), pp. 153–169.

4 J. Hattie and H. Timperley, 'The Power of Feedback', *Review of Educational Research*, 77(1) (2007), pp. 81–112.

5 C. Dweck, *Mindset-Updated Edition: Changing the Way You Think to Fulfill Your Potential* (Hachette, 2017).

6 P. J. Black and D. Wiliam, 'Classroom Assessment and Pedagogy', *Assessment in Education: Principles, Policy and Practice*, 25(3) (2018).

7 H. Andrade, 'Using Rubrics to Promote Thinking and Learning', *Educational Leadership*, 57(5) (2000), pp. 13–18.

8 H. Andrade, 'Self-Assessment Through Rubrics', *Informative Assessment*, 65(4) (2007), pp. 60–63.

9 T. Groenendijk, F. Haanstra and A. Kárpáti, 'Self-Assessment in Art Education Through a Visual Rubric', *International Journal of Art & Design Education*, 39(1) (2020), pp. 153–175.

10 O. Maarleveld and H. Kortland, 'Beeldend reflecteren: een nieuwe beoordelingsmethode voor praktisch beeldend werk in het voortgezet onderwijs' [Visual Reflection: A New Assessment Method for Studio Art in Secondary Education], in F. Haanstra (ed.), *Beoordelen in de kunstvakken: instrumenten en onderzoek* (Amsterdamse Hogeschool voor de Kunsten, 2020).

11 Ibid.

12 A. Kárpáti and Z. Paál, 'Assessment of Visual Sub-Competencies Through Visual Rubrics: Case Studies Based on the Common European Framework of Reference of Visual Competencies (CEFR-VC)', *Journal of Visual Literacy*, 41(3) (2022), pp. 1–23.

13 Ibid.

14 T. Groenendijk, F. Haanstra and A. Kárpáti, 'Self-Assessment in Art Education Through a Visual Rubric'.

15 A. Kárpáti and Z. Paál, 'Assessment of Visual Sub-Competencies Through Visual Rubrics: Case Studies Based on the Common European Framework of Reference of Visual Competencies'.

16 P. Dunbar-Hall, J. Rowley, W. Brooks, H. Cotton and A. Lill, 'E-Portfolios in Music and Other Performing Arts Education: History Through a Critique', *Journal of Historical Research in Music Education*, 36(2) (2015), pp. 139–154.

17 Ibid., p. 147.

18 J. M. Silveira, 'Portfolios and Assessment in Music Classes', *Music Educators Journal*, 99(3) (2013), pp. 15–24.

19 G. Hughes, 'Towards a Personal Best: A Case for Introducing Ipsative Assessment in Higher Education', *Studies in Higher Education*, 36(3) (2011), pp. 353–367.

20 R. J. Stiggins, 'Assessment Literacy', *Phi Delta Kappan*, 72(7) (1991), pp. 534–539.

21 D. Sluijsmans, D. Joosten-ten Brinke and C. Van der Vleuten, *Toetsen met leerwaarde. Een reviewstudie naar de effectieve kenmerken van formatief toetsen* [Learning from assessment: a review of effective features of formative assessment]. (NWO-PROO, 2013).

22 E. Soep, 'Assessment and Visual Arts Education'.

23 L. Lindström, 'Creativity: What is it? Can You Assess It? Can It Be Taught?', *Journal of Art & Design Education*, 25(1) (2006), pp. 53–66.

24 J. Ross, 'The Reliability, Validity and Utility of Self-Assessment', *Practical Assessment, Research & Evaluation*, 11(10) (2006), pp. 1–13.

25 T. Groenendijk, F. Haanstra and
    A. Kárpáti, 'Self-Assessment in Art
    Education Through a Visual Rubric'.
26 J. Ross, 'The Reliability, Validity and
    Utility of Self-Assessment'.
27 D. Sluijsmans, D. Joosten-ten Brinke
    and C. Van der Vleuten, *Toetsen met
    leerwaarde. Een reviewstudie naar de
    effectieve kenmerken van formatief
    toetsen*.
28 D. R. Sadler, 'Formative Assessment
    and the Design of Instructional
    Systems', *Instructional Science*, 18
    (1989), pp. 119–144.
29 L. Price, 'Peer Evaluation (or "No,
    you can't say Jimmy sucks.")', www.
    theatrefolk.com/blog/peer-evaluation.
30 L. Green, Meaning, *Autonomy and
    Authenticity in the Music Classroom,
    inaugural professorial lecture*
    (Institute of Education, University
    of London, 2005).
31 E. Van Hoek, 'Bandcheck',
    Kunstzone 4 (2017), pp. 6–8.

Chapter 8

Curriculum Evaluation

Nicole Eisenman (1965) is an American figurative artist who makes paintings, drawings, sculptures and installations about social and political situations, gender, racism, and technology. Eisenman uses elements and styles from art history and pop culture. The painting *Selfie* shows how we study and evaluate ourselves.

Most teachers make 'curriculum selfies' to evaluate their curricula. They observe when things go well or when they do not go as expected. This can lead to minor or even major changes, or in rare cases even to the conclusion that the curriculum is flawless! This kind of evaluative activities mostly happen in an informal and somewhat unsystematic way. But sometimes it is wise to do a more thorough curriculum evaluation, for instance when you and your colleagues have developed a whole new one. Or, perhaps when teaching a certain course has become a routine and a fresh and critical look is needed.

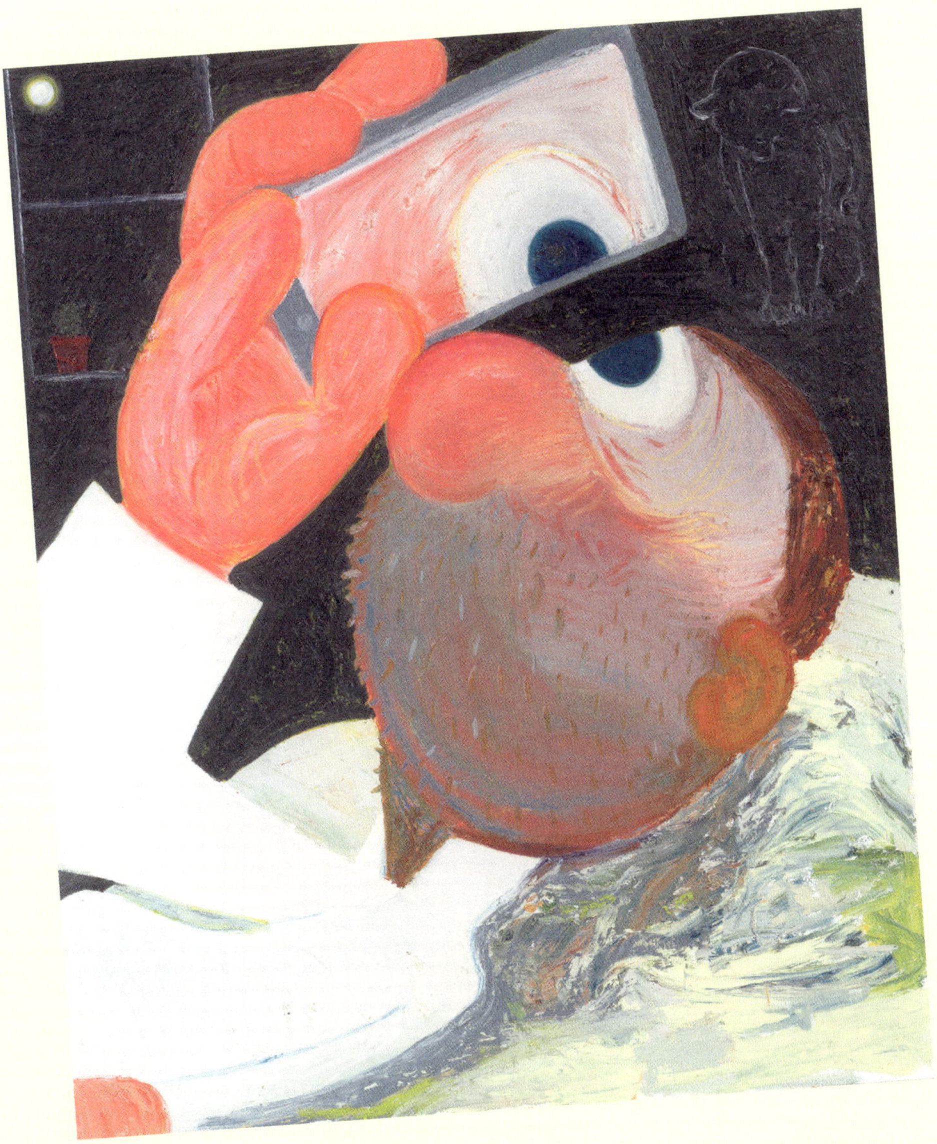

Nicole Eisenman, *Selfie* (2014)

Contents of this chapter

8.1 What is Curriculum Evaluation?

We can define curriculum evaluation as a method for collecting, analysing and interpreting information about the effectiveness and value of curricula. Educational evaluation helps to determine how a curriculum works and what could be improved. As with the assessment of students' learning there is a distinction between formative and summative evaluation. Formative evaluation is meant to improve the curriculum, while it is being carried out. In summative evaluation, the effects of a curriculum are evaluated after it has been put into practice. Evaluation of the curriculum is a continuous activity; therefore, curriculum design and evaluation are complementary processes. There are various strategies and methods that can be used to conduct educational evaluations. We will discuss two systematic ways of curriculum evaluation: the use of student evaluations and the use of a specific evaluation model.

8.2 Student Evaluations

An obvious way to evaluate a curriculum is to ask the opinion of the learners. For instance, you can have a group discussion with your students. When the group is small this can be a good way, but when the group is large not all students can share their views. Moreover, in a group discussion it is more difficult to be critical than when you can give your opinion in an anonymous way. Therefore, students' summative evaluations also come in the form of questionnaires. Students can be asked to give general opinions on a course or project: Did they think it was useful? What did they like and what didn't they like? Were they satisfied with the teaching? A questionnaire can even be more specific and ask a number of questions about different aspects, for instance about the assignments, the teaching, the group interaction or the assessment of the course or project. See the table on page 163 for an example.

As for learning, one can simply ask: Did you attain the learning goals of the course? Or you can list all the goals of a course and ask for each whether a student did attain them or not, or only partly. Another possibility is to pose an open question about the learning process: What did you learn from this course? Students then have to complete a number of sentences beginning with: I have learned that... or I have learned how... This form of so-called learner reports is interesting as it provides information on what students consider their most important learning experiences.[1] Moreover, students can learn more or other things than are formulated in the goals. You also can invite students to mention attitudinal aspects, personal experiences: I have learned that I ....

A particular form of student evaluation is the student rating of teaching. This is a commonly used method for evaluating teaching in higher education, but much less widely applied in primary and secondary education. The student rating focuses on teacher behaviour and contains items such as: Teacher is prepared for class; Teacher knows their subject; Teacher provides activities that make content matter meaningful; Teacher allows you to be active in the classroom; Teacher gives me good feedback; Teacher grades fairly, and so on. However, the validity of student ratings of teaching is debated, because they are influenced by many factors not attributable to teaching, such as the teacher's personality.[2,3] Therefore, students do not always learn more from more highly rated teachers. We think that we should take the students' opinions seriously, just like in self-assessments. But student evaluations should not be limited to teacher behaviour and they should not be a sole measure of the quality of a taught and learned curriculum.

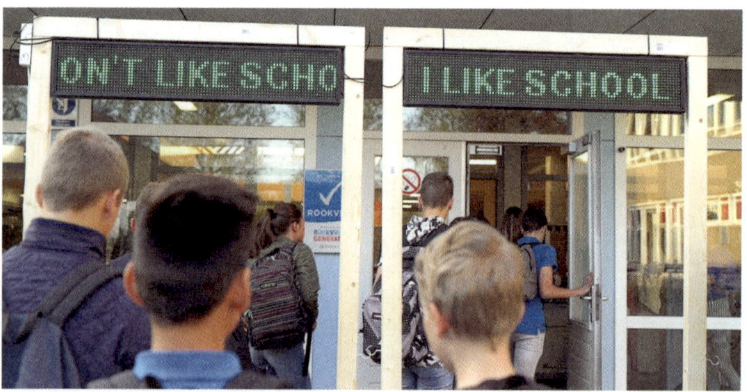

Authentic Boys, *I Don't Like School, I Like School* (2017–2019). During their residency at a secondary school, arts collective Authentic Boys satirically assessed how students judged their school by choosing a positive or negative answer. Result: ca. 5 per cent liked school, 95 per cent did not

Course evaluation survey

Your opinion on the course is very valuable to me. Please note that your evaluation is anonymous and that I won't see the results until after the grades for the course are given.

Course title: ....

	Strongly agree	Agree	Disagree	Strongly disagree
I was prepared for this course / I had enough knowledge to start this course				
I found there was enough variety in activities during the course (instruction, discussion, making, etc.)				
I found the assignments challenging				
The assignments gave me enough freedom				
I had enough materials/instruments/ props/ ... to do the assignments				
I had enough time to complete the assignments				
The teacher gave me good feedback				
My peers gave me good feedback				
The way the assignments/course was assessed was clear to me				
The way the assignments/course was assessed was fair				

Open questions:
- What assignment did you like most and why?
- What assignment did you like the least and why?

What did you learn from this course:
- I learned that/how/ ....
- What did you miss in this course?

General comments ....

Example of a course evaluation survey for students

8.3 Evaluating Your Curriculum with an Evaluation Model

The most systematic way to evaluate a curriculum is to make use of an evaluation model. There are several evaluation models in circulation, but in general they have been developed for evaluation research and are used by external evaluators. An example is the extensive evaluation of a music course by music teachers in sixteen primary schools in Amsterdam.[4] The evaluators used a model that provided tools for context, input, process, and product evaluation. The researchers collected data through observations, question-naires, interviews, and self-reports of music teachers. In the evaluation report, the researchers provided recommendations on how to improve the music curriculum. The scope of such an evaluation and its length (three years) are clearly not feasible for teachers. However, already in 1967 Robert Stake proposed a model that is useful as a tool for teachers who want to evaluate their own courses or curricula (see figure below).[5]

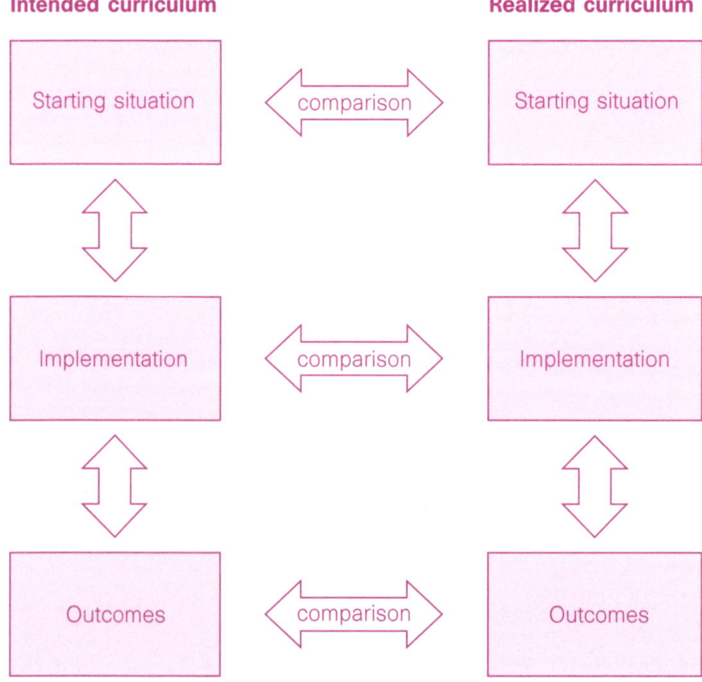

Adaption of evaluation model of Robert Stake (1967)[6]

In short, this model is based on the comparison of what has been planned (the intended curriculum) and what is realized (the implemented and the attained curricula). As explained in the paragraph about curriculum manifestations in chapter 1, only seldom do teachers realize all that is intended. The comparison in Stake's model concerns three major curriculum areas: the starting situation, the implementation, and the outcomes of a curriculum. The starting situation includes the student's prior knowledge, skills, and attitudes but also teacher expertise, materials, and facilities. The implementation concerns all activities during the course or project such as assignments, learning activities, the way the curriculum is structured, assessments, etc. The outcomes are the learning results of the students.

In the intended (written) curriculum there has to be a plausible relationship between the intended starting situation, the implementation, and the kind of learning outcomes. The realized curriculum (that what is implemented and what learning outcomes are attained) will show how the relationships have worked out.

Comparing the Intended and Realized Curriculum

The evaluation starts with comparing the intended and the realized curriculum, as is illustrated in the table on page 164.

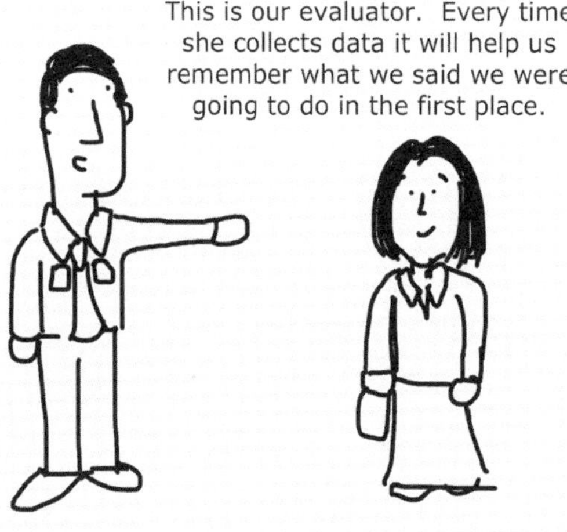

The Evaluator on freshspectrum.com

In Stake's model this comparison consists of three steps:

- The first step in evaluation involves a comparison between the intended and the actual starting situation: did you make a good estimation of the prior knowledge and competencies of your students. Were the desired equipment, instruments, materials, studios, etc. available?
- The second step in evaluation is a comparison between the intended and the realized curriculum. The former includes everything that the teachers and students intended to do, the latter includes what has actually happened. There often is a discrepancy between the two as it is difficult to cover all of the intended lesson content and carry out all of the intended learning activities. A related question is whether the structure of the curriculum is appropriate and the available time is sufficient.
- The third and last comparison answers the main question of the evaluation: did the curriculum result in the desired outcomes? The formative and the summative assessments of students learning are the main input here. You could say that if the majority of students have shown proficient learning results the answer to the main question is affirmative. But there are more issues you can look at. An important fact is whether the range in outcomes is very large (from insufficient to very advanced) or is it small and have most students scored sufficient on the criteria. Other information comes from looking at the outcomes for the different criteria. Are there certain criteria that are more difficult to meet than others? Or, if the course consists of several assignments, it makes sense to look at differences in outcomes between these assignments.

The above comparisons describe if and to what extent there are discrepancies between what was intended and what is realized and describes characteristics of the realized curriculum. But an evaluation has to go beyond description and has to provide an explanation and a judgment as well.

Explaining Differences Between
the Intended and Realized Curriculum

Now you must analyse and try to explain *why* things did or did not go as planned. And subsequently, what this means for the effectiveness and the practicality of the curriculum, for such conclusions will guide improvement decisions. It is important to note that in order to come to such conclusions you have to interpret the gathered information. As judgment criteria can vary between teachers, there is a subjective element to this. One teacher can find a sufficient score of more than half of the students satisfactory; another may find this result too meagre. The latter teacher will look for ways to improve this score, the former will leave the curriculum unchanged.

For making this appraisal you not only have to compare components of the intended and the realized curriculum, but you also have to pay attention to the connections between starting situation, implementation, and outcomes. In the figure on page 164 this means not only looking at the horizontal arrows, but also the vertical ones. For instance, when the realized outcomes are not satisfactory, you should try to find out whether this was because some features of the intended starting point were not met. Did you underestimate or overestimate the prior competencies of the students? Did your assignments connect to their interests? Were some facilities or materials missing during the course?

Or you can relate outcomes with implementation. Did you give enough information about the goals and the context of the assignments? Did you implement only part of the learning activities and if so, why? Was there enough time for the students to go through the different phases of making a performance or product? Was there a good balance between openness and structure in the assignments?

And when judging the desired and realized outcomes: Were some criteria unclear or were some criteria neglected? For instance, the resulting products or performances may be original and conceptually adequate, but lacking in technical execution.

8.4 Informal or Systematic Evaluation?

Although formative and summative assessments of students'
learning have different goals than curriculum evaluation, they
are important sources of information for judging the curriculum.
Even more so when teachers not only give feedback to students,
but also the other way around. And of course, when student
evaluations took place the results are important data as well. Based
on all these judgments, you can make changes in your curriculum,
changes in the requirements of the starting situation, changes in
aspects of the assignments and learning activities, changes in the
curriculum structure, or changes in the assessment and assessment
criteria. It can also influence your teaching: do the students need
more information and demonstration? Is more individualized
teaching required?

Like mentioned before, informal forms of evaluation during
or at the end of a course mostly will provide enough information
to judge the merit of a curriculum. Systematic evaluations are
time-consuming and frequent student evaluations will be taken less
seriously by the students. But from time to time a more thorough
and systematic approach to curriculum evaluation is desirable.

8.5 Design Result: Your Curriculum's Strengths and Weaknesses

When you decide to evaluate your curriculum in a systematic way
you can, for instance, collect information by group interviews
with students or student evaluation questionnaires. You can also
use a complete evaluation model, involving a comparison of the
different aspects of the intended curriculum on the one hand and the
implemented and attained curriculum on the other hand. You will
interpret the information and conclude if changes in the curriculum
are called for.

Next Up?

Now that we have discussed the evaluation of the curriculum, has the design process come to an end? No, we have made clear already that curriculum design is a continuing process. The outcomes of the evaluation can make you return to certain phases and elements of the design.

NOTES

1   A. D. De Groot, 'Wat neemt de leerling mee van onderwijs?' [What Do Students Gain From Education?], in *Handboek voor de onderwijspraktijk: deel 2* (Van Loghum Slaterus, 1980), pp. 2.3 Gro. A1-24.
2   S. Jimaa, 'Students' Rating: Is It a Measure of an Effective Teaching or Best Gauge of Learning?', *Procedia — Social and Behavioral Sciences*, 83 (2013), pp. 30-34.
3   B. Uttl, 'Lessons Learned from Research on Student Evaluation of Teaching in Higher Education', in W. Rollett et al. (eds.), *Student Feedback on Teaching in Schools* (Springer, 2021), pp. 237-256.
4   J. Herfs and E. van Hoek, *Muziekles is anders* [Music Lessons Are Different] Aslan Muziekcentrum 'de Muziek Talent Express' Een doorlopende leerlijn voor muziekonderwijs in de basisschool 2010-2013 (Amsterdamse Hogeschool voor de Kunsten, 2013).
5   R. E. Stake, 'The Countenance of Educational Evaluation', *Teachers College Record*, 68, (1967), pp. 523-540.
6   Ibid.

Epilogue

You have reached the last pages of this book. By now, you and your colleagues will have followed the different design phases, and have hopefully made a slice of curriculum that is fresh, tailor-made and satisfying to your students. The workbook provided the cooking methods, but you collaboratively, creatively and systematically came up with your own unique Wicked Arts Curriculum. A curriculum that challenges your students to reflect on themselves, the arts, and the world.

During the design process, we hope you experienced that the arts are an endless source of inspiration for your curriculum design. By visiting exhibitions, films, concerts, theatre and dance performances, you can keep on topping up your glass of ideas for curricula, projects, and courses — simply go and taste what is out there! Moreover, do not forget to keep on connecting to your students' preferences and to keep on enlarging your taste palette. Society at large, too, has a mixture of political, provocative, or poetical themes on offer that can invigorate your curriculum. There is so much inspiration out there — enough for a lifetime of designing.

So, although this is really the end of the book, it should not be the end of your creative, artistic, and collaborative design process. Be inspired by Rirkrit Tiravanija: keep on working in that kitchen of *Wicked Arts Education* and keep on coming up with surprising, tasty curricula!

Next Up?
Start all over again.

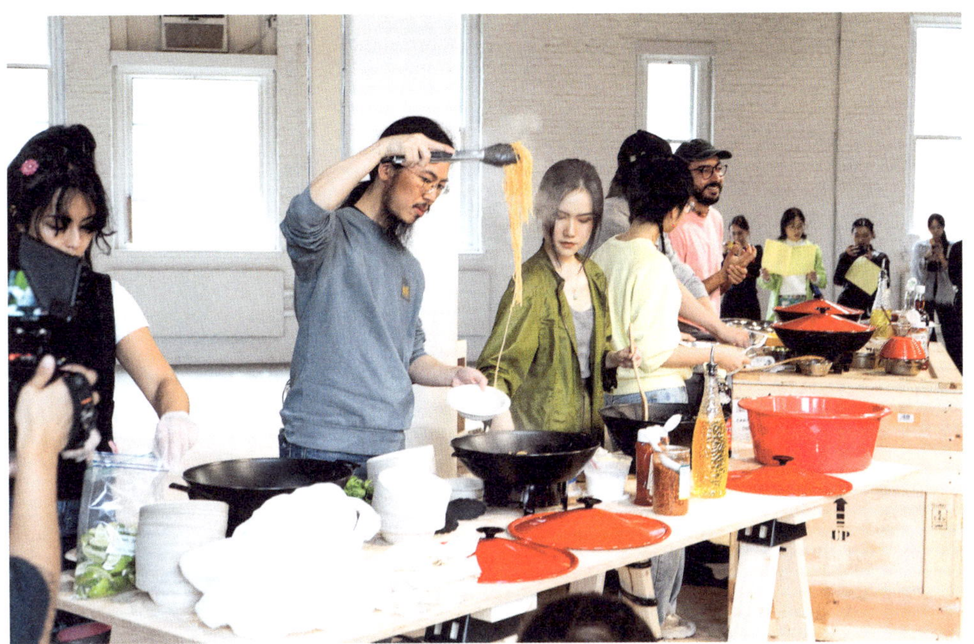

Rirkrit Tiravanija, *Free* (1992). The artist Rirkrit Tiravanija has used shared food in his work for many years. In 1992 he converted a gallery in New York into a kitchen where he served rice and Thai curry for free. In 2012 the artist worked with MoMA to recreate the experience. For Who's afraid of red, yellow and green, first exhibited in Bangkok in 2010 and in 2019 in the Hirshhorn Museum and Sculpture Garden, Tiravanija had a popular local restaurant to prepare and present three curries—red, yellow and green. The installation included a large-scale mural, which referenced protests against Thai government policies

Appendix

MULTIDISCIPLINARY RUBRIC
WICKED ARTS EDUCATION

This instrument is meant to help with the (self)assessment of your skills in describing and judging arts products or arts performances

ARTS APPRECIATION

Recognizing style, genre and function

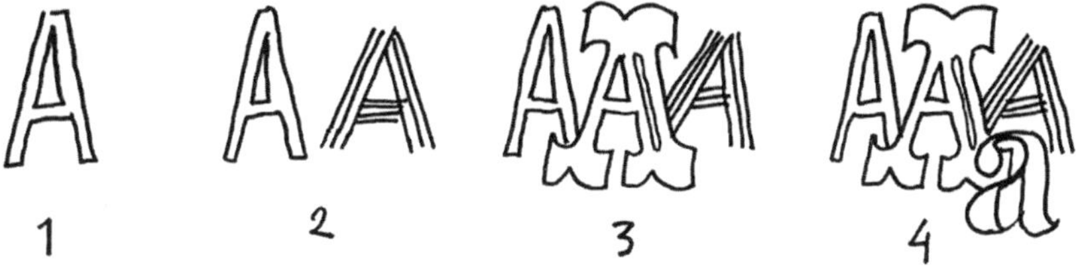

Interpreting

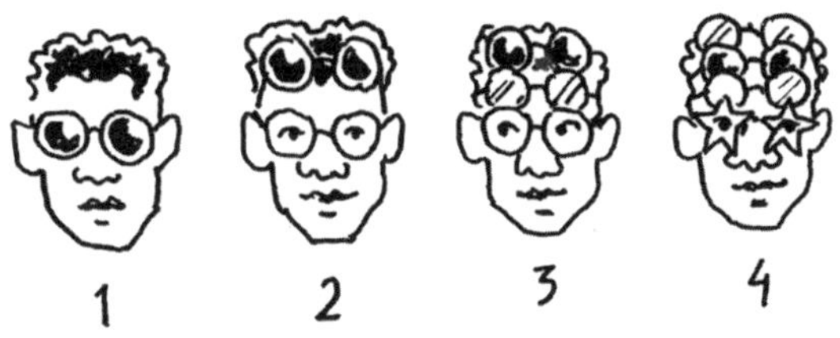

Expressing a considered opinion

Collecting sources of inspiration

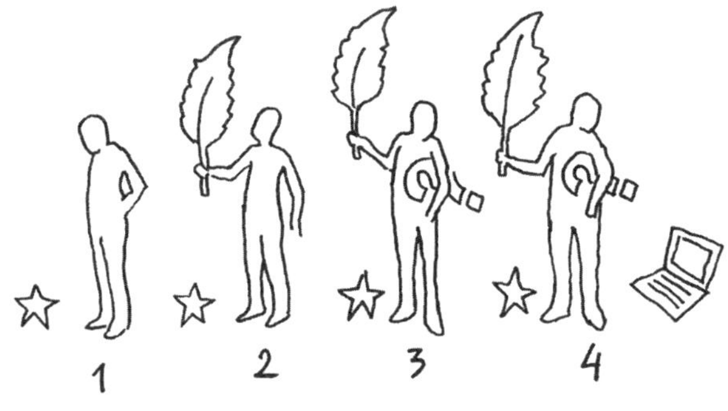

Exploring ideas

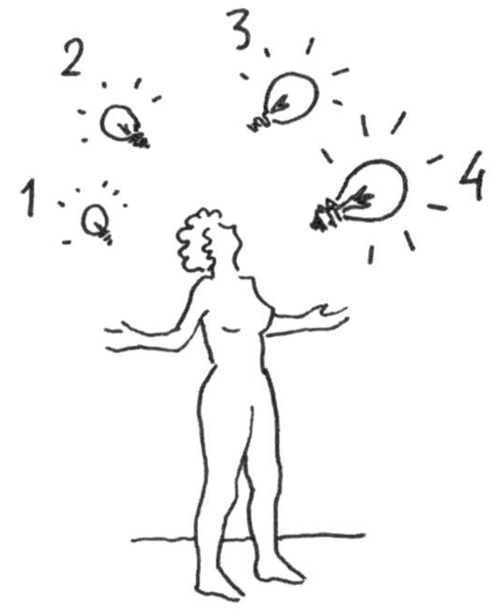

Experimenting

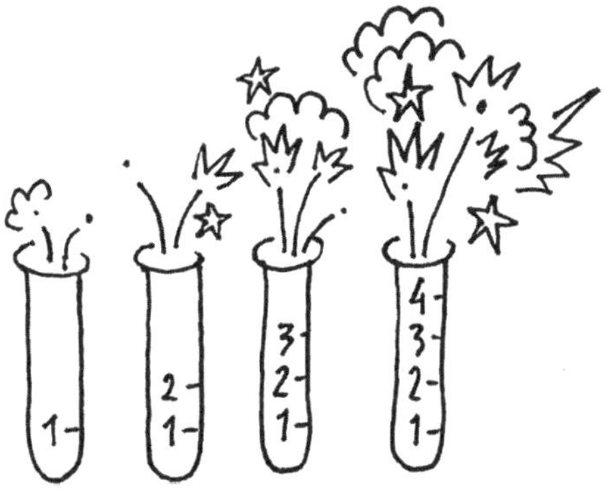

ARTS PRODUCTION

Using technical skills

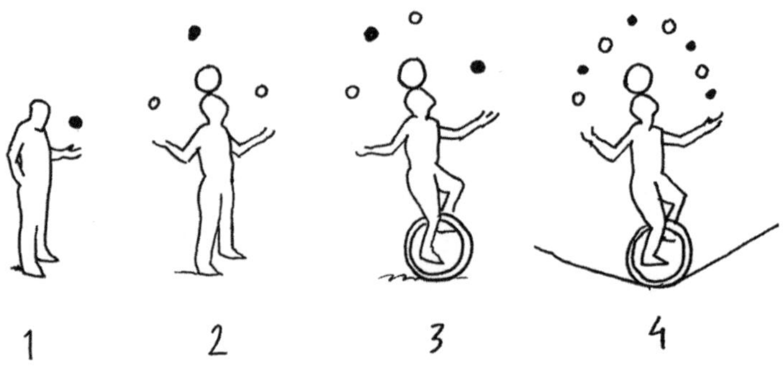

Persevering

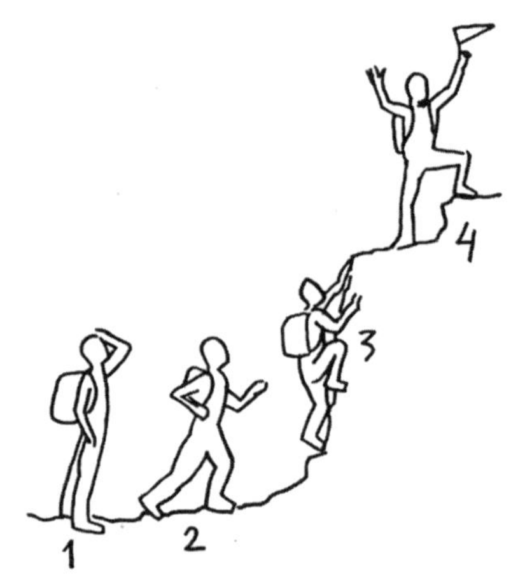

Collaborating

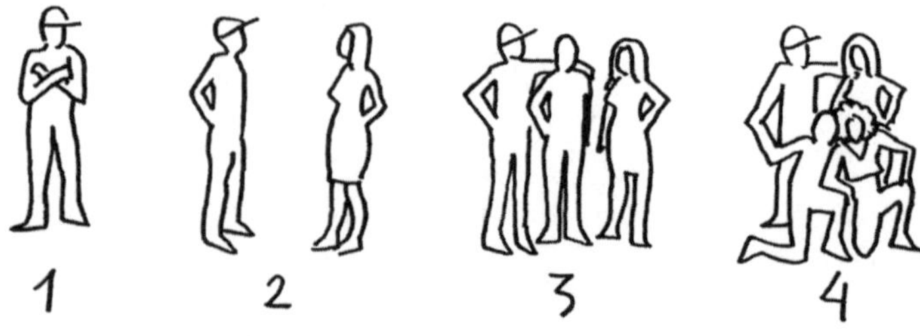

PRESENTATION AND PERFORMANCE

Presenting / performing

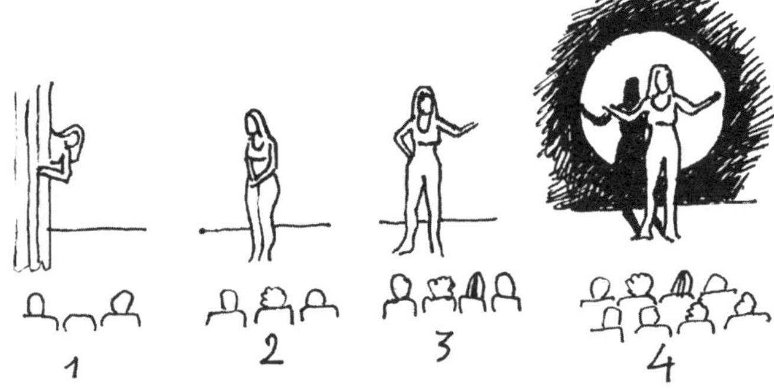

Explaining your work

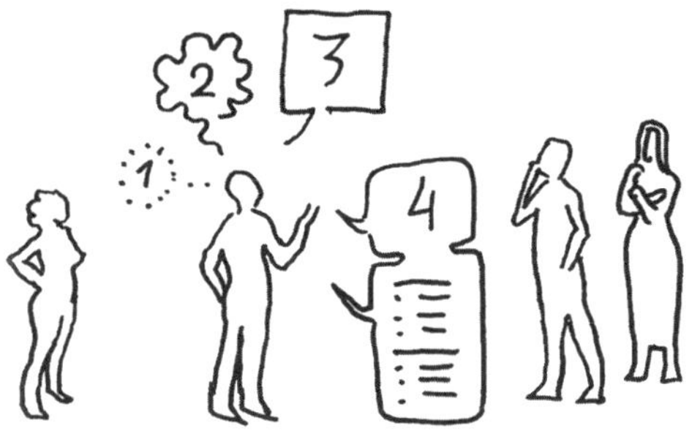

ARTS APPRECIATION

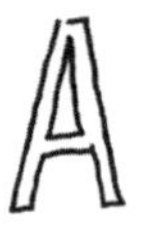 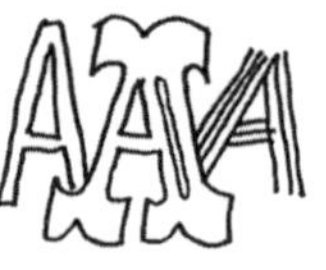 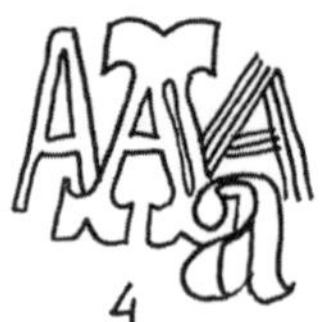

Criteria	1	2	3	4
Recognizing style, genre and function	You barely recognized styles, genres or functions. You did not describe them clearlycand you did not use arts specific vocabulary.	You recognized some styles, genres or functions. You described them by using little arts specific vocabulary.	You recognized several, styles, genres and functions. You described them clearly by using arts specific vocabulary regularly.	You recognized many styles, genres and functions. You described them clearly by using arts specific vocabulary consistently.

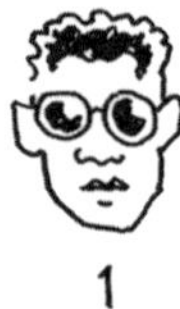 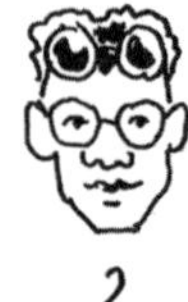 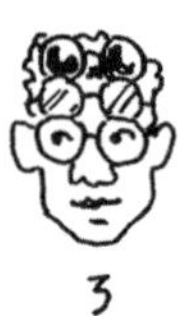 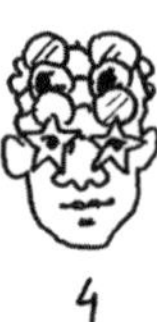

Criteria	1	2	3	4
Interpreting	You interpreted the products or performances only through one lens or your personal perspective. The interpretation is not convincing/plausible.	You interpreted the products or performances through two lenses or perspectives. These interpretations are convincing/plausible.	You interpreted the products or performances through three lenses or perspectives. These interpretations are convincing/plausible.	You interpreted the products or performances through more than three lenses or perspectives. The interpretations are convincing/plausible and surprising/original.

Criteria	1	2	3	4
Expressing a considered opinion	Your opinion is unconsidered and lacks arguments.	Your opinion is somewhat considered and is hardly founded on arguments.	Your opinion is considered and is founded on some arguments.	Your opinion is considered thoughtfully and is well founded on various argument.

RESEARCH

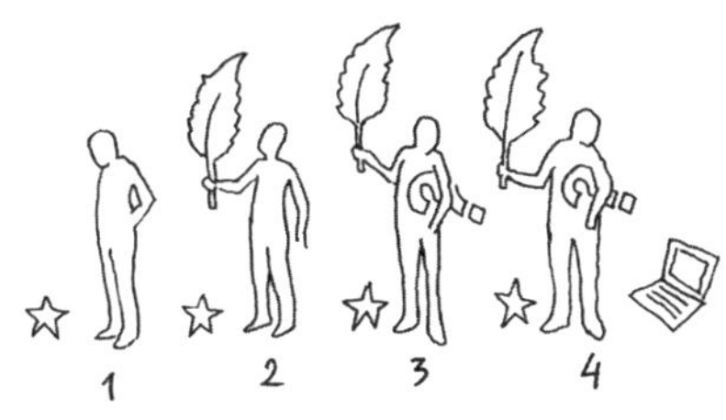

Criteria	1	2	3	4
Collecting sources of inspiration	You collected almost no sources of inspiration and you did not study (e.g by sketches or notes) a theme to work on.	You collected a few sources of inspiration to study (e.g by sketches or notes) a preliminary theme to work on.	You made an extensive collection of sources of inspiration to study (e.g by sketches or notes) one theme in depth to work on.	You made an extensive and varied collection of sources of inspiration to study (e.g by sketches or notes) several themes in depth to work on.

Criteria	1	2	3	4
Exploring ideas	You explored the first idea that came to mind.	You randomly explored several ideas before you started producing.	You purposefully explored several ideas within a theme and chose the one that seemed promising.	You deeply explored several ideas within a theme. You deliberately chose the one that was most promising.

Criteria	1	2	3	4
Experimenting	You started directly to produce your final product. You did not try out different concepts, materials, techniques, or methods.	You took a little time experimenting. You tried one or two concepts, materials, techniques, or methods, but it is unclear how this relates to your final work.	You took time experimenting. You tried out several concepts, materials, techniques, or methods, which helped you to create your final work.	You took a lot of time experimenting. You tried out a broad range of concepts, materials, techniques, or methods, as well as unusual possibilities, resulting in discoveries you used in your final work.

ARTS PRODUCTION

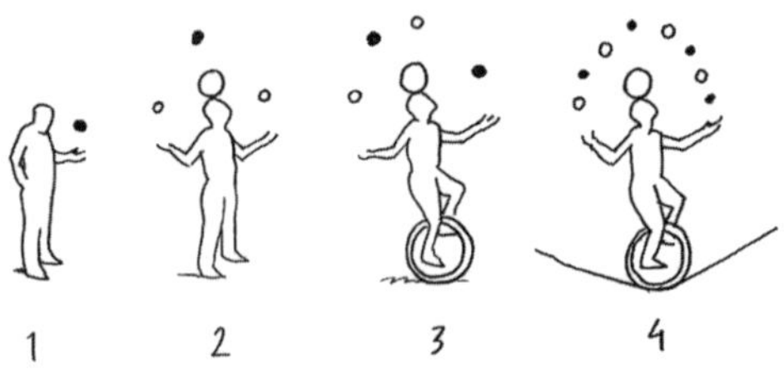

Criteria	1	2	3	4
Using technical skills	Your product or performance suffers from a lack of technical skills.	Your product or performance would be optimized with the use of more technical skills.	Your product or performance benefits from your technical skills.	Your product or performance is enhanced by the excellent use of technical skills.

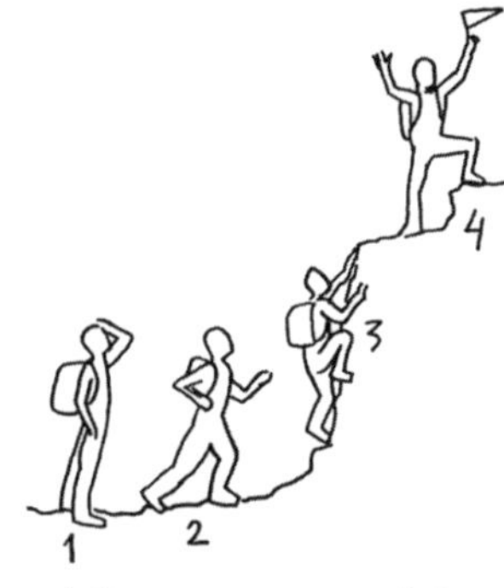

Criteria	1	2	3	4
Persevering	When something did not work, you gave up.	When something did not work, to keep going, you needed the teacher to solve a problem.	When something did not work, to keep going, you tried it again.	When something did not work, to keep going, you tried it again, and solved problems yourself or with your peers.

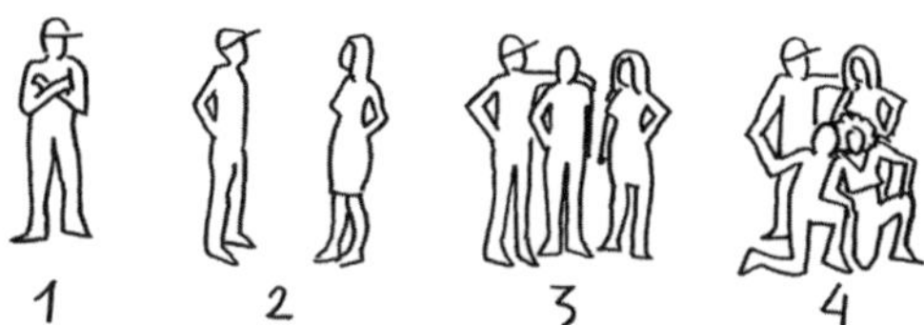

Criteria	1	2	3	4
Collaborating	You preferred to work alone and barely interacted with others in the group.	You preferred to work alone, but you interacted with others in the group Sometimes you listened to others.	You worked together with others. You often felt responsible for the group work, mostly listening to others. Sometimes you took the initiative.	You made an effort to work together and learn from others. You felt responsible for the group work, actively listening to others. Often you took the initiative.

PRESENTATION AND PERFORMANCE

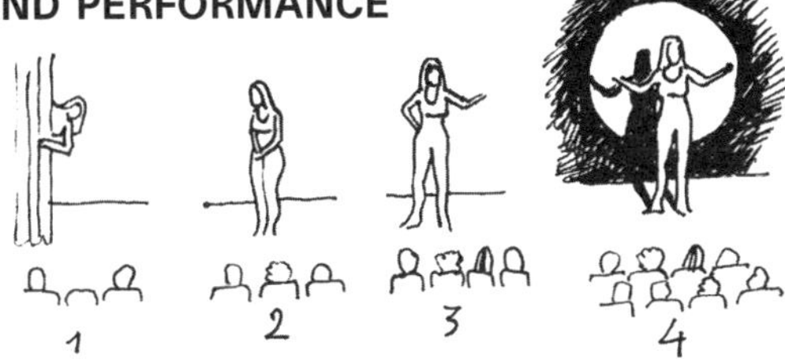

Criteria	1	2	3	4
Presenting/ performing	Your presentation or performance is unconvincing and distorted the meaning of the work.	Your presentation or performance is slightly convincing but it only partially strengthened the meaning of your work.	Your presentation or performance is convincing and the meaning of the work came across.	Your presentation or performance is extremely convincing and amplifies the meaning of your work.

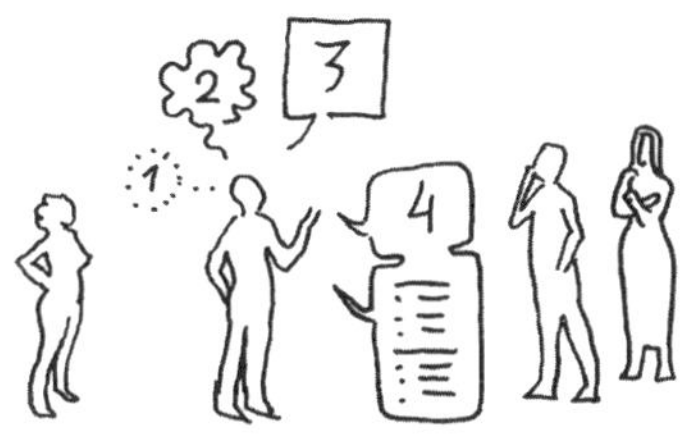

Criteria	1	2	3	4
Explaining your work	The explanation of your work was not understandable. You did not explain form and content of the work.	The explanation of your work was partly understandable. You explained a few aspects with regard to form or content of the work.	The explanation of your work was broadly understandable. You explained most aspects with regard to form and content of the work.	The explanation of your work was fully understandable. You explained all important aspects with regard to form and content of the work.

Design Model for Wicked Arts Curricula

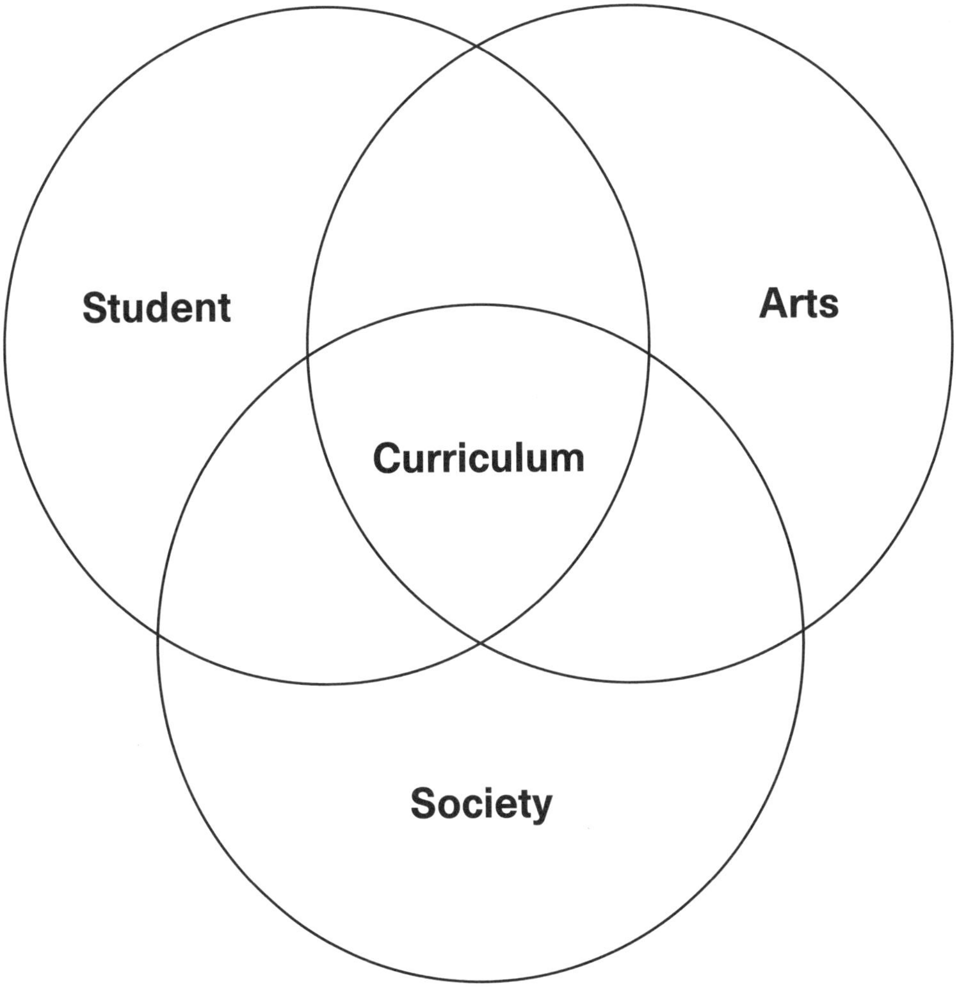

You can find more worksheets and handouts here:

Index

Wicked Arts Education

Index

Credits of the Images

p. 162 Authentic Boys, *I Don't Like School, I Like School* (2017–2019), collaboration Theater Artemis, Den Bosch, NL/Design Museum Den Bosch, NL, photo: Melanie Pardoel. Ten different artists stayed at nine secondary schools, for three days and three nights. Filmmaker Melanie Pardoel created a documentary of every performance.

p. 30 JooYoung Choi, *Like a Bolt out of the Blue, Faith Steps in and Sees You Through* (detail) (2019). This detail is featuring Poundcake Man, Emma Poundcake Girl and Lady Madness; wooden armature, fabric and hardware, paint, vinyl dots, photo: Thomas R. DuBrock, courtesy of Inman Gallery, Houston, TX. The Korean-American artist uses video, painting, photography, and sculpture. Her inspiration comes from her personal experiences, the media of her childhood, her ongoing research on identity and American media's representation of girls, women, intersex, transgender, and non-binary people of colour.

p. 93 Driessens & Verstappen, *Tickle Salon 2.0* (2018), work in progress, robotic installation, made on assignment for the Niet Normaal Foundation, for the project and exhibition 'Robot Love'.

p. 159 Nicole Eisenman, *Selfie* (2014), oil painting on canvas, 134.6 × 111.8 cm, photo: Robert Wedemeyer. Eisenman's vibrant cartoonish paintings and drawings explore themes like humanity, queerness and society.

p. 94 left Frances Glessner Lee, Police murder scene scale model (ca 1944). American forensic scientist Glessner Lee (1878–1962) crafted these miniature crime scenes to train homicide investigators to 'convict the guilty, clear the innocent, and find the truth in a nutshell'. The 'Nutshell Studies' are still used in forensic training today.

p. 137 Naomi He-Ji, *Once Upon a Ball* (2021). Ballroom is a form of protest. Ballroom 'houses' offer safety, love and guidance to lhbti+ people of colour. Pictured, Guilliano Pinas encourages dancers on the catwalk during 'Once Upon a Ball', Maassilo Rotterdam, 6 November 2021.

p. 21 Annette Kraus, *Hidden Curriculum* (2007–). Using performance and film as tools, the artist playfully explores with students the transformative potential of (un)learning. At Whitechapel Gallery she collaborated with A level students from St Paul's Way Trust School, Tower Hamlets, London and GCSE students from Cumberland School in Newham, London.

p. 105 Anouk Kruithof, *Universal Tongue* (2021), view from the solo exhibition 'Universal Tongue', Kunstencentrum VIERNULVIER (formerly Vooruit), Ghent, BE, 2021, photo: Niccolò Quaresima.

p. 110 Gabriela Lang, *Performative guided tour through ZKM (Centre for Art and Media)* (2023), © ZKM | Center for Art and Media, photo: Fidelis Fuchs.

p. 151 BA LaRue / Alamy Stock Photo. Three teenage boys who have formed a garage band, practice music in a garage in Oklahoma City, Oklahoma, USA.

p. 72 Maider López, *Polder Cup*, 2010, 4th September, 2010. Ottoland, NL, produced by Witte de With Center for Contemporary Art and SKOR/Foundation Art and Public Space, NL.

p. 22 Małgorzata Mirga-Tas, *Re-enchanting the World* (detail), (2022), installation, textile and acrylic on canvas, on wooden frame, 462 × 387 cm, photo: Bartek Solik. The title is inspired by Silvia Federici's book, *Re-enchanting the World: Feminism and the Politics of the Commons* (2018), which proposes re-enchanting as a way of recovering the idea of community and rebuilding relationships with others, including non-human actors: animals, plants, water or mountains.

Credits of the Images

p. 60 M.I.A., *Bad Girls* (2012), video still. *Bad Girls* is a song by British recording artist M.I.A. from her fourth studio album *Matangi* (2013). It can be seen as a social commentary on women positions, in this case in solidarity with the 'Women to Drive' movement in Saudi Arabia. The song was written by Maya 'M.I.A.' Arulpragasam, Marcella Araica and Floyd Nathaniel 'Danja' Hills, and produced by Danja.

p. 115 Jennifer New, *Drawing from Life: The Journal as Art* (Princeton Architectural Press, 2005)

p. 67 Pedro Noguera, *Reality, Equality, Equity, Justice* (2022). For forty years American sociologist and educator Pedro Noguera has been fighting racial inequality in education. He wants all American students, of every ethnic and economic background, to benefit from equal opportunity.

p. 87 Reezky Pradatop, Top view of gamelan instruments, Java, Indonesia (2020). Alamy Stock Photos

p. 116 Julia Risler and Pablo Ares (Iconoclasistas), *Harvest Map of a Neighbourhood of Mexico City, Mexico* (2012). The Iconoclasistas' collective mapping workshops utilize techniques of Marxist pedagogy, while bringing attention to visual ideologies and ways spatial relations shape consciousness.

p. 15 Julian Rosefeldt, *Manifesto* (2015), video still from the 13-channel film installation. Each of the thirteen screens presents the same actor (Cate Blanchett) taking on various roles: schoolteacher, homeless man, factory worker, puppeteer, scientist. All of the monologues are formed out of various artists' manifestos published over the last 150 years.

p. 77 Richard Serra, *Verb List*, 1967, pencil on two sheets of paper, each 25.4 × 21.6 cm. *Verb List* is a handwritten list of 108 verbs, all in Serra's precise cursive. The verbs are active, and imply a task, a movement or a process.

p. 53 Max Siedentopf, *Slapdash Supercars*, 2015, series of photographs (each edition of 25), C-Print, 28 cm × 20 cm.

p. 139 Ghita Skali, *Relentless Putridity* (2023), intervention with a wooden door containing hatches from the past of Prix de Rome, whitening product smell (certified fragrance), pamphlet, dispenser, brick wall. Pamphlet's design: Roxanne Maillet; production research: Dana Claansen; scent developed by International Flavors & Fragrances (IFF); scent mechanism: Jorg Hempenius, Iscent; pamphlet stamper: Nolwenn Vuillier; with the support of the Shoulder Warmers Committee.

p. 119 Keri Smith, *The Guerilla Art Kit: Everything You Need to Put Your Message out into the World* (Princeton Architectural Press, 2007).

p. 67 Asefeh Tayabana, *Precious Burden*. The artist strives to build a connection between jewellery as an aesthetic expression and jewellery as a means to convey messages. With her set of *Precious Burden* objects she is trying to show a glimpse of what it means to be autistic.

p. 171 Rirkrit Tiravanija, *Free* (1992), courtesy: Rirkrit Tiravanija Archive, Berlin.

p. 79 Hans Traxler, *Chancengleichheit* (1983) (Equal chances) in: Michael Klant (ed.), *Schul-Spott: Karikaturen aus 2500 Jahren Pädagogik* (Fackel-träger-Verlag, 1983), p. 25.

p. 58 Erik Van Hove, *V12 Laraki* (2013), mixed media, 53 materials, 180 × 150 × 150 cm, 380 kg, courtesy Hood Museum of Art, Dartmouth College, Hanover, NH (USA).

p. 62 Mart Veldhuis, *Eigen Schuld* (2021), jacquard-woven wool (woven by EE Exclusives), acrylic, cotton and polyester, 150 × 470 cm. The goal was to hang the tapestry in a government building to encourage politicians to consider the consequences of the study loan system.

p. 112 Wang Qingsong, *Follow Me (Lesson Eight)* (2003), HD video, duration 1:00. Wang set up a large blackboard (4 × 8 m) at Beijing Film Studios. He covered it with Chinese and English slogans reflecting the changes in Chinese history, culture and society, related to the economic growth of recent decades.

Biographies

Authors

Melissa Bremmer is a professor of Arts Education at the Amsterdam University of the Arts. She completed her Bachelor in Music Education at the Conservatory of Amsterdam, her Master in Educational Science at the University of Amsterdam and obtained her PhD at the University of Exeter. Her research focuses on *Wicked Arts Education*, Embodied Music Pedagogy, music education & disability, and ArtsSciences education.

Emiel Heijnen is a professor of Arts Education at the Amsterdam University of the Arts. He has worked in various contexts as an arts and design teacher and obtained his PhD at the Radboud University Nijmegen. His research focuses on interdisciplinary arts education, popular culture/media education, curriculum design, and ArtsSciences education. Emiel teaches the courses 'Arts Educational Design' and 'Teaching as Artistic Practice' at the Master of Education in the Arts in Amsterdam.

Folkert Haanstra studied Psychology and Fine Art in Groningen. He held the special chair for Cultural Education and Cultural Participation at the University Utrecht and was Professor of Arts Education at the Amsterdam University of the Arts. His research focuses on the effects of arts education and student assessment in the arts.

Co-editor

Sanne Kersten is coordinator and researcher at the Research Group Arts Education of the Amsterdam University of the Arts. Her research focuses on ArtsSciences education and Neurodiversity and she previously worked on research regarding the theme of the 'Teacher as Conceptual Artist'. She is also coordinator of the third cycle program THIRD and has extensive experience in publishing books.

University of the Arts Amsterdam

The Research Group Arts Education of the Amsterdam University of the Arts is focused on developing knowledge, designing research-based curricula and innovating professional practices in the field of arts education. It publishes and organizes symposia and events around two main research strands: Interdisciplinarity and Social Engagement. www.ahk.nl/en/research-groups/research-group-arts-education/

Designer

Laura Pappa is a freelance graphic designer based in Amsterdam. Her clients include Valiz, Van Abbemuseum, Nieuwe Instituut, Rozenstraat — a rose is a rose is a rose, Kunstverein Toronto, and the Museum of Estonian Architecture. She teaches Graphic Design at the Estonian Academy of Arts in Tallinn. www.laurapappa.biz

Publisher

Valiz is an independent international publisher and addresses contemporary developments in art, design, urban affairs, and visual culture. Their books offer critical reflection and interdisciplinary inspiration in a broad-based and imaginative way, often establishing a connection between cultural disciplines and socio-economic questions. Valiz is based in Amsterdam and connects to authors, artists, designers, institutes, bookshops, distributors, and readers worldwide. www.valiz.nl

Colophon

Authors: Melissa Bremmer,
    Emiel Heijnen, Folkert Haanstra
Co-editor: Sanne Kersten
Project editor Valiz: Eli Witteman
English copy-editing: Leo Reijnen
Proofreading and index: Vivi van Leersum
Illustrations: Oskar Maarleveld
    (pp. 142–143, 174–181)
Design: Laura Pappa
Typefaces: Neue Haas Unica,
    Century Expanded
Paper inside: Munken Print White 90 gr. 1.5
Paper cover: Invercote 200 gr.
Lithography: KOLORworkx, Koog aan de Zaan
Printing and binding: Wilco, Amersfoort
Publisher: Valiz, Amsterdam, Astrid Vorstermans
    www.valiz.nl

Acknowledgements
The authors thank all members of their
critical reading team: Allerd van den Bremen,
Clark Goldsberry, Talita Groenendijk, Jorge
Lucero, Joost Overmars, Maren Siebert,
Wieke Teselink.

This project was generously supported by the

 **Amsterdam University of the Arts**

Distribution
NL /LU: Centraal Boekhuis, www.cb.nl
Belgium: EPO, www.epo.be
Europe (excl UK/IE, NL, BE)/Asia:
Idea Books, www.ideabooks.nl
GB/IE: Central Books, www.centralbooks.com
USA, Canada, Latin America:
D.A.P., www.artbook.com
Australia: Perimeter,
www.perimeterdistribution.com
Individual orders: www.valiz.nl, info@valiz.nl

This book has been printed on FSC-certified
paper by an FSC-certified printer. The FSC,
Forest Stewardship Council promotes
environmentally appropriate, socially beneficial,
and economically viable management of
the world's forests. fsc.org

This publication is also available in
a Dutch-language version:
Melissa Bremmer, Emiel Heijnen, Folkert
Haanstra, *Wicked Kunsteducatie: Creatieve
programma's ontwerpen* (Amsterdam:
Valiz, 2024), ISBN 978-94-93246-39-3

Also available:
Emiel Heijnen, Melissa Bremmer, *Wicked
Arts Assignments: Practising Creativity in
Contemporary Arts Education* (Amsterdam:
Valiz, 2020), ISBN 978-94-92095-75-6

Wicked Arts Education, this English edition:
ISBN 978-94-93246-38-6
Printed and bound in the EU, 2024